Places to Amaze You!

by Grace Hansen

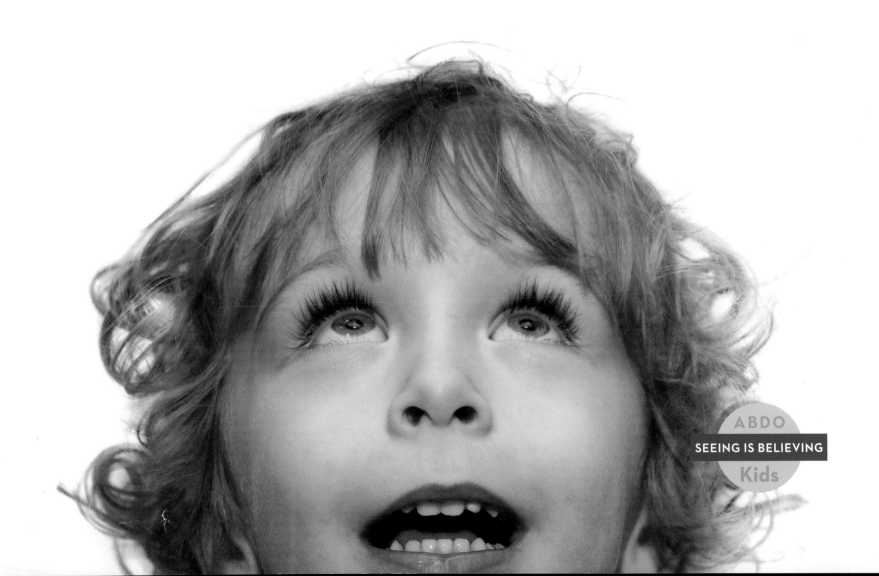

ABDO
SEEING IS BELIEVING
Kids

abdopublishing.com

Published by Abdo Kids, a division of ABDO, PO Box 398166, Minneapolis, Minnesota 55439.

Printed in the United States of America, North Mankato, Minnesota.

102014

012015

 THIS BOOK CONTAINS
RECYCLED MATERIALS

Photo Credits: Corbis, Glow Images, iStock, Shutterstock

Production Contributors: Teddy Borth, Jennie Forsberg, Grace Hansen

Design Contributors: Laura Rask, Dorothy Toth

Library of Congress Control Number: 2014943788

Cataloging-in-Publication Data

Hansen, Grace.

 Places to amaze you! / Grace Hansen.

  p. cm. -- (Seeing is believing)

ISBN 978-1-62970-733-4

Includes index.

1. Landforms--Juvenile literature. 2. Travel--Juvenile literature. 3. Curiosities and wonders--Juvenile
literature.   I. Title.

910--dc23

                    2014943788

Table of Contents

The Netherlands

The Netherlands has many

tulip fields. They are colorful.

They bloom every spring.

4

5

Alaska, USA

The Mendenhall Glacier ice cave
is in Alaska. The cave is under
a 12-mile (19 km) **glacier**!

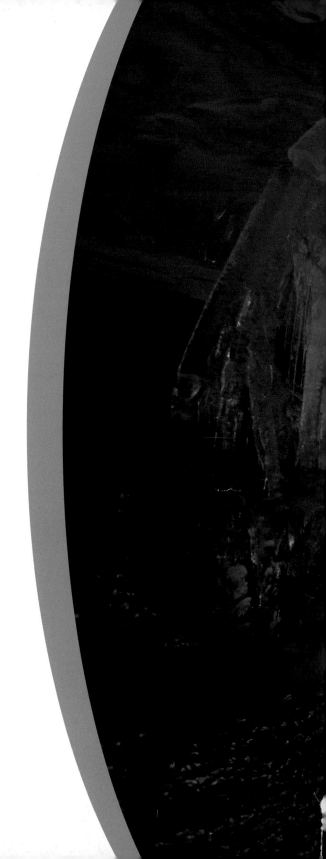

Arizona, USA

Antelope Canyon is in Arizona.

It was formed by flowing water.

9

Maldives

The Sea of Stars is in the
Maldives. Small animals
in the water light up.
They glow like stars.

11

Turkey

Cappadocia is in Turkey. People like to hot air balloon here. Water flow created the waving rocks.

13

Croatia

Plitvice Lakes National Park is in Croatia. There are many caves and waterfalls.

Bolivia

Salar de Uyuni is in Bolivia.

It is the world's largest **salt flat**.

It can mirror the sky.

17

Iceland

The Silfra rift is in Iceland. It is part of the **Atlantic rift**. Divers swim between two **continents**!

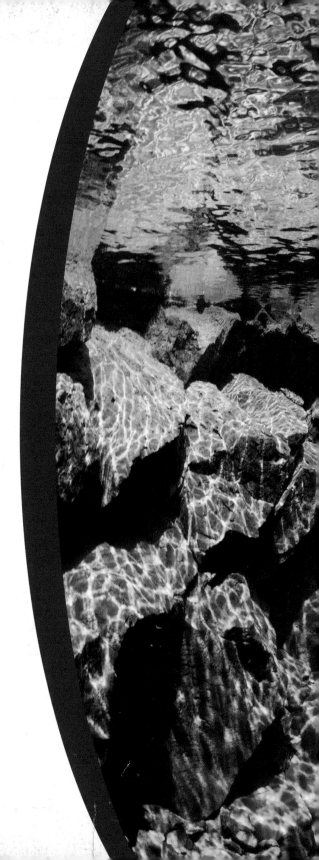

19

Australia

The Great Barrier Reef is amazing. It is off the coast of Australia. It is very big. You can see it from space!

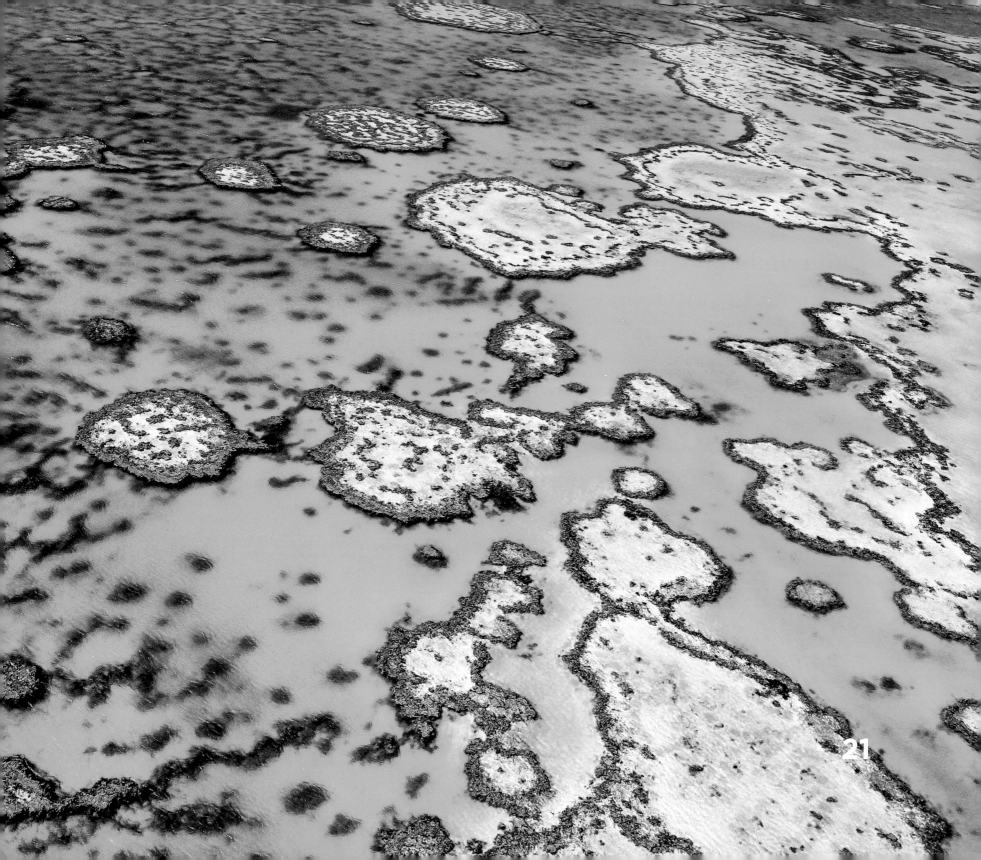

More Facts

- The Netherlands is known for its tulips. The Netherlands sends Canada 10,000 tulip bulbs each year. It is to thank them for their help in World War II, which ended in 1946.

- Cappadocia is a Turkish fairy-tale town. The view from above is amazing. But even more amazing is what is underground. There are miles of tunnels and rooms. It is called the Underground City.

- The Great Barrier Reef is home to a huge number of plants and animals. Over 1,000 species of fish live there. Over 1,000 coral reef species live there. Sea turtles, starfish, whales, dolphins, and much more live there too!

Glossary

Atlantic rift – a large crack that separates the Eurasian and North American plates. The crack goes right through Iceland.

continent – one of the seven main landmasses on Earth. The seven are Europe, Asia, Africa, North America, South America, Australia, and Antarctica.

glacier – a very big piece of ice that moves slowly.

salt flat – a desert lake where water has completely dried up leaving high amounts of shiny salts.

Index

abdokids.com

Use this code to log on to abdokids.com and access crafts, games, videos, and more!

Abdo Kids Code:
SPK7334

Contents

Introduction

DELTA Business Communication Skills is a new series which uses a learner-centred approach to develop key communication and language skills essential for today's international business environment. The series is designed for learners of business English at pre-intermediate and intermediate level, either pre-service or in-service, and it can be used either in the classroom or for self-study.

Features of the series include:

- Individual Needs analysis and Learning journal
- Awareness-raising activities
- Extensive personalized exercises
- Tips for effective performance in business
- Helpful suggestions for language study
- Regular language reference and review sections
- Photocopiable resources
- An integrated audio CD
- Full transcripts and answer key

E-mailing aims to help you to develop the skills and language you need to write effective business e-mails in English. *E-mailing* consists of six core units, each containing:

- **Context** – to raise awareness of the skills and issues involved in each stage of the e-mail writing process, and to introduce different strategies for developing these skills
- **Presentation** and **Practice** – of core language (vocabulary, grammar and phrases) linked to these skills
- **Tips** (cultural or language related) – for e-mailing effectively
- **Consolidation** – to allow you to apply what you have learned to your own work situation
- **Reference** – useful vocabulary and phrases related to each unit
- **Review** – study suggestions and further practice (ideal for homework/self-study)

The book also contains:

- **Needs analysis**. This encourages you to consider what you need to focus on in order to get the most out of the book and your learning.
- **Learning journal**. This provides the opportunity to reflect and personalize what you have studied in the book.
- **Resources section**. This provides additional material such as checklists, photocopiable frameworks and additional activities.
- **Answer key**. This includes suggested answers and is designed to enable you to work either alone or with a teacher.
- **Transcripts**. These detail the content of the accompanying CD.

How to use this book

Step 1

Start by working through the **Needs analysis** (page 5). This will help you to:

- consider the e-mails you write in English – and your strengths and weaknesses in writing these;
- identify and prioritize your immediate and future needs for writing e-mails;
- determine the order in which you work through the core units in this book.

I hope you enjoy learning with this book.

Louise Pile

Louise Pile
Series editor and author

Step 2

You should then familiarize yourself with the **Learning journal** (pages 6 and 7). You are asked to refer back to this journal at the end of every core unit.

Step 3

Work through the units in the order that you feel is most appropriate to your needs.

About the author

Louise Pile has extensive Business English teaching and teacher-training experience, both in the UK and abroad. She has written and edited a range of print and multimedia language-learning materials.

Needs analysis

Nowadays, most of us send and receive e-mails regularly – in both our personal and business life – but few of us take the time to stop and consider for a moment whether we are 'effective e-mailers'. Just because we do something a lot doesn't make us good at it. Stop and consider for a moment the e-mails you write in English, and how good you think you are at writing them, by completing the questionnaire below. You will focus on all areas in this Needs analysis in more detail in this book.

Questionnaire

1 On average, how many e-mails do you:
receive every day? ❑   send every day? ❑

2 Of those e-mails you send, how many are in English?
about ¼ ❑   about ½ ❑   about ¾ ❑
nearly all ❑   other: ..... ❑

3 What is the ratio of e-mails you send in English to people outside your company (external) and those working in the same company (internal), e.g. 70:30?

4 Who do you write business e-mails in English to?

5 What are your main reasons for writing?

6 What e-mail system do you use (e.g. Outlook), and what features does it have (forward/delete/filter, etc.)?

7 What percentage of the e-mails that you receive each day have real information value for your work?

8 On average, how much time do you spend a day preparing e-mails?
< 10 minutes ❑   10–20 minutes ❑
20–30 minutes ❑   > 30 minutes ❑

9 What percentage of the e-mails that you send or receive each day could actually be dealt with more efficiently on the phone or at a meeting?

10 Does your company have an e-mail policy/guidelines (e.g. outlining company policy on appropriate style to use when e-mailing)?
Yes ❑   No ❑

11 What do you find easy/difficult about writing e-mails in English?

12 What do you think makes an e-mail *more* effective (e.g. being short) and *less* effective (e.g. full of mistakes)?

13 What do you think you do well/need help with?

Prioritizing your needs

Each unit of *E-mailing* focuses on a different area. Look through the unit summaries at the beginning of Units 1–6 and think about which areas you need to develop.
Developing your awareness of what you already do well and what you could do better will allow you to focus on improving those skills you really need.

Step 1
Note down the units you would like to work through in order of priority for you, in terms of the area in which you feel you are weakest, or which is currently of most importance to you.

Step 2
Discuss and agree with your teacher the order in which you will work through the units.

Priority	Unit number and focus area
1	
2	
3	
4	
5	
6	

Step 3
Before you start working through the units – in the order you have decided on – look at the Learning journal on pages 6 and 7.

Learning journal

During the course

As you work through each unit, summarize helpful language and tips for effective e-mailing. An example is given, but what you note down will depend on your own learning pattern.

Example

Unit: 6

Useful language: to do your best; to make a reservation; to run a spell check; to attend a session; I've worked here since 1999/for three years.

Useful tips: check my e-mail will make a good impression on the reader; ask Jon to read through my e-mail before sending it

Your Learning journal

Unit: 1 **Useful language:** **Useful tips:**	**Unit:** 2 **Useful language:** **Useful tips:**
Unit: 3 **Useful language:** **Useful tips:**	**Unit:** 4 **Useful language:** **Useful tips:**
Unit: 5 **Useful language:** **Useful tips:**	**Unit:** 6 **Useful language:** **Useful tips:**

After the course

You will have made progress already, but it is important to consolidate your learning, both during your course and at work.

After you have completed each unit, decide how you will continue to develop your skills, for example, which review exercises you will do or how you will practise what you have learned in the workplace. Note that it is helpful to give yourself realistic deadlines!

Make notes on developing your skills, for example, using a framework like the one below. An example is given to help you.

Example

Unit: 3

Focus area: Writing clear and concise e-mails

I need to:
explain any complicated and technical terms the reader might not know;
I also need to check I have not given any unnecessary detail/information.

To do this better, I intend to:
do all review exercises (15th March); I will also ask my colleague to read my next e-mail to my boss and give feedback before I send it.

Your planner

Unit:

Focus area:

I need to ...

To do this better, I intend to ...

This book is designed to be used during and after a course, so keep it with you and refer back to it whenever you need to, and keep adding to your notes!

Getting started

THIS UNIT LOOKS AT:

■ **key e-mail terminology and 'netiquette'**

■ **language for beginning and ending e-mails**

■ **giving your reason for writing**

■ **referring to previous and future contact**

netiquette *n.* /'netɪket/ The unwritten rules of behaviour on the Internet, especially related to the use of e-mail, chat rooms and newsgroups.

Context

1 **Look at the e-mail below and consider these questions.**

1 Who is the sender? the receiver?

2 Is there a signature? a disclaimer?

3 Is the subject line filled in?

4 Has the importance option been used?

5 Has the e-mail been copied to anyone else (using the *bcc* (blind carbon copy) or *cc* (carbon copy) field)?

6 What is the purpose of the e-mail?

7 What format would the attachment be in?

8 What is the receiver expected to do?

> To: p-vogel@mply.de
> From: s.griffin@travelexpress.com
> Cc:
> Bcc:
> Subject: Sales Manager post (ref. 7672P)
>
> Dear Mr Vogel
>
> Thank you for your e-mail expressing interest in the above vacancy.
>
> Please confirm whether you would prefer to receive an application form and further details by e-mail (Word XP, approximately 55K) or in hard copy by post.
>
> If you have any questions, please do not hesitate to e-mail or phone me.
>
> Yours sincerely
>
> Stacey Griffin
> Personnel Assistant
> s.griffin@travelexpress.com
>
> Travel Express
> 35 Windmill Street
> Evesham EM2 9TR
> UK
> Tel: +44 (0)1868 767565 (extn 392)
> Fax: +44 (0)1868 767600
>
> ***************
> http://www.travelexpress.com
> The content of this e-mail and any attachments sent with it are confidential and for the addressee only. Any unauthorised copying or distribution by anyone else is prohibited. Please delete this e-mail if you have obtained it in error.

Tips
• Update the contact details in your signature regularly.
• Include **http://** in the website address – not all e-mail systems will treat it as a live link otherwise.

2 a Think of the last business e-mail you received.

● Who was it from?

● What were you expected to do?

b Think of the last e-mail you sent.

● Who was it to?

● What was your reason for writing it?

Presentation
Best practice guidelines

1 Some companies have guidelines on how staff should use e-mail. Look at the following extract from the guidelines of Travel Express. Complete the gaps using words from the Context section.

Getting the basics right!

1 Make sure you have the _____'s e-mail address correct. It's easy to send an e-mail to the wrong person!

2 Use the _____ only if someone else needs to be kept informed or to take action.

3 Include the following information in your _____ : your name, job title, company name and address, telephone number.

4 The company's website address and a legal _____ are sometimes automatically added to all outgoing messages.

5 Ensure the _____ clearly describes what the e-mail is about and is free of errors.

6 Do not use *Reply all* unless you mean to e-mail the whole group.

7 Use the body of the e-mail if possible. If you do need to send an _____ , first check with the receiver that the format (*Word*, etc.) and file size are appropriate.

8 Use the *bcc* field instead of the _____ field to avoid having large numbers of names in the e-mail header, and to avoid making e-mail addresses known to other people.

9 Only use the _____ (high priority) if your e-mail requires quick action, or if others need to receive information from you urgently.

10 Don't forward e-mails unless the sender has given you permission.

2 How useful do you consider these guidelines to be? If your company has guidelines, how similar/different are they to those above?

3 ∩ 1.1 For more practice on getting addresses right, do the exercises on page 56 in the Resources section.

4 Look at the example e-mails below. To what extent does each follow the guidelines on page 9?

1

To:	e_jason@kuhn.co.uk
From:	myra-wynn@sales.try.com
Subject:	hi

 Trylawn_leaflet.pdf

Dear Ms Jason
Thank you for your phone call of 3rd January. I am pleased to hear that Model BHT43 has been selling well. I am attaching a leaflet listing our full range of lawnmowers, as requested. I look forward to doing business further with you in the future.
Yours sincerely

Myra Wynn
Sales Assistant

2

To:	Leila-Rajala@iho.fi
From:	boris@mistra.com
Subject:	meeting next week

Dear Leila
I just wanted to let you know that I can make the product launch next week.
Give me a ring if you need any help to organize the event.
Best wishes
Boris

3

To:	info@shal.com
From:	Michaela_Salter@can.com
Subject:	

I am writing to you in response to your advertisement in 'Cycling weekly'. I am interested in stocking your forthcoming Model 232 and would be grateful if you could send me further information about this range.
Best regards
Michaela Salter
Buyer

Bimleys
15 High Street
Sinton SI4 5BH

4

To:	martin_summersby@ht.com
Cc:	s_sandhu@mk-mode.de
Bcc:	
From:	m.schmidt@mk-mode.de
Subject:	catalogue request

MKcat.pdf

Dear Mr Summersby
Further to your e-mail of 12th September, I would like to apologize for the delay in sending you our sales catalogue. We have just put together our new catalogue and I wanted to be able to send you the most up-to-date information about our products. Please find attached a PDF of our latest catalogue.
If you require any further details about any of the items listed, please do not hesitate to contact me by e-mail or phone.
Yours sincerely
Markus Schmidt
Customer Services Officer
MK Mode
Tel: +49 (0)7531 3859
http://www.mk-mode.de
****
The content of this e-mail and any attachments sent with it are confidential and for the addressee only. Any unauthorised copying or distribution by anyone else is prohibited. The views expressed here are not necessarily those of the company.

Tip To keep an e-mail focused, try to have just one purpose.

5 Look at the phrases below. Then find additional phrases in the e-mails on page 10 to add to the table.

Giving the reason for writing	Making reference to previous contact	Making reference to future contact
We wish to (inform you of a change to our prices). Just wondered if (you could help me). * I am writing in reply to / concerning / with regard to / about (your latest brochure). Just a quick e-mail to (say hi). * I am writing to (remind you about the sales conference).	With reference to (our recent phone call), ... In reply to (your letter), ... I was really glad to hear (about your job). * I refer to (your last e-mail). I saw (your advertisement in the local paper). We understand from your e-mail that (you are interested in) ... Nice to hear from you yesterday. *	Drop me a line some time. * I hope to hear from you shortly. If you would like any additional information, please do not hesitate to contact us. Give me a call later on. * If you have any questions, please e-mail or phone me. I enjoyed meeting you and look forward to (working with you on the project).

* informal phrase

6 Match the reasons for writing to the opening phrases below.

1 inviting   1 a   Just wondered if you'd like to ...*

2 apologizing   5 b   On behalf of Sandra Jameson, I would like to thank you for ...

3 informing   2 c   I wish to apologize for not ...

4 requesting   3 d   I'm writing to ask if you could ...

5 thanking   6 e   I am writing to complain about ...

6 complaining   4 f   This is just to let you know that ...*

7 Think of different ways of completing the reasons for writing in Exercise 6.

8 Match these greetings and endings. Do you use any of these when e-mailing? If so, in which situations? What other greetings and endings do you use and in which situations?

Tips
- Think about who you're writing to and how they expect to be addressed.
- Formal business e-mails generally follow the same style as the greetings and endings of business letters.

1 Dear Mr/Mrs/Miss/Ms Gillet   4 a   [*Your name*]

2 Dear Finn/Margit   1 b   Yours sincerely

3 Hi, Mike   3 c   Bye for now

4 John: 2 d   Best regards

1 Match these key terms with their definitions.

1 netiquette *c*
2 subject line *a*
3 attachment *e*
4 to cc someone in *g*
5 signature *d*
6 format *b*
7 in-tray *f*

a where you write the topic of your message
b type of electronic file (e.g. Word)
c good-practice guidelines for e-mailing
d your contact details below your e-mail
e a document e-mailed to someone
f a folder containing messages for you to read
g to copy your message to another person

2 Put the words in the correct order to form sentences.

1 your dated I writing am reply in to letter 5 June
2 look I forward to your receiving reply
3 please attached find a copy catalogue of our
4 you thank for e-mail your
5 you if have questions any please not do hesitate contact to me
6 I writing am concerning the launch product week next
7 really I'm the glad to about interview hear
8 if you wondered like to just meet would up later

3 Complete the e-mail using words and phrases from the Presentation section.

> To: elene_martina@usel.com
> From: p.harmer@ut.fr
> Subject: USEL'S product range
>
> 1_____ Ms Martina
>
> I am writing 2_____ regard 3_____ your advertisement in *Business Weekly*.
> I would be grateful if you 4_____ send me some information about your latest product range.
> I 5_____ forward to 6_____ from you shortly.
>
> Yours 7_____
> Petra Harmer

4 🎧 1.2 **Listen to a voicemail message from a colleague. Make notes in the framework on page 56 of the Resources section. Then write the e-mail.**

5 **You are Lars Hansen from Copenhagen. You receive the following e-mail. Look at the notes and write your reply. Before you reply, consider again the questions in the framework on page 56 of the Resources section.**

To: hansen.l@hei.com
Cc: j_franklin@reer.com
From: p_ronneberg@reer.com
Subject: Price list: electrical goods

 Attachments:

price_list.doc

Dear Mr Hansen

Thank you for your enquiry of 2nd February. I have attached a price list for our new range of electrical goods, as requested.
Please note that Jason Franklin, our sales representative for Scandinavia, will be in Denmark next week for a trade fair. He would be pleased to visit you in Copenhagen to discuss any of our products.
If you would like any further information, please do not hesitate to contact me.

Yours sincerely
Per Ronneberg

Maybe meet Mr Franklin on Tuesday?

Do they have a brochure on frost-free fridges?

Payment terms?

Consolidation

1 a **Think of an e-mail you need to write for business. Make notes on the questions in the framework on page 56 of the Resources section.**

b **Write your e-mail.**

Tip Keep in mind the purpose of your e-mail – and what you want to happen as a result of it.

2 **Reread the e-mail from the reader's point of view. Is there anything you would now change?**

→ NOW TURN TO YOUR LEARNING JOURNAL AND MAKE NOTES ON THIS UNIT.

Reference   *Useful phrases*

Greetings

Dear Mr/Mrs/Ms/Miss Gillet

Dear Sir; Dear Sir/Madam; Dear Madam

Dear Finn/Margit

Hello Mike *

Hi Jane *

Endings

Yours sincerely

Yours faithfully

Best regards / Best wishes

All the best *

Bye for now *

Reasons for writing

I am writing in reply to / concerning / with regard to / about (your latest brochure).

Just wondered if you could (help me). *

I am writing to (remind you about the sales conference).

We wish to (inform you of a change to our prices).

Just a quick e-mail to (say hi).*

I am writing in response to your advertisement.

I would like to (attend the seminar).

I just wanted to let you know (that I can make the product launch). *

This is just to (say thanks for your e-mail). *

Referring to previous/future contact

With reference to (your phone call), ...

In reply to (your letter), ...

Nice to hear from you. *

Thank you for your phone call.

Further to (your e-mail of 12th September), ...

I hope to hear from you ...

Give me a call later on. *

If you would like any further/additional information, please do not hesitate to contact us.

I was really glad to hear (about the successful launch).*

I look forward to doing business with you again in the future.

Drop me a line some time.*

I refer to (your last e-mail).

I saw (your website).

We understand from your e-mail that ...

If you have any questions, please e-mail or phone me.

I enjoyed meeting you and look forward to (meeting you soon).

Vocabulary

Key e-mailing terminology

to attach / an attachment

to forward (an e-mail)

disclaimer

format

importance option

live link

receiver/addressee/recipient

signature

subject (line)

Sales and marketing

advertisement

catalogue

direct mail

distribution

enquiry

launch

leaflet

marketing seminar

payment terms

price list

promotional materials

range

sales (representative/conference, etc.)

trade fair

* informal

Review

1 What do you need to consider when writing an e-mail?

- *your reason for writing*
-
-

2 Complete the gaps in this e-mail with a word or phrase from the unit.

> To: karen.steiner@phs.com
> From: j.vogt@intermark.de
> Subject: Marketing seminar
>
> Dear Ms Steiner
> 1 _____ your telephone call on 13th July.
> 2 _____ confirm that I am able to attend the direct mail marketing seminar
> next week. Please could you 3 _____ if I need to bring any examples of our
> promotional materials, such as leaflets or brochures?
>
> 4 _____
> Johannes Vogt
> Marketing Assistant

3 Write a short e-mail to a friend:

- referring to an e-mail he/she sent;
- inviting him/her for lunch;
- asking him/her to confirm the arrangement.

4 How many words in the unit can you find to do with sales/marketing?

SALES/MARKETING

5 Write an e-mail to a company requesting a brochure in response to their recent advert in the local paper. Remember to provide your contact details.

Study suggestion

Keep a record of new terms/words with their definition, e.g.
subject line = where you write the topic of your message
addressee = the person receiving your e-mail
to cc someone into an e-mail = to send a copy of your message to someone else
attachment = a document sent to someone using e-mail
in-box/in-tray = a folder containing messages for you to read
signature = your contact details below your e-mail

UNIT 2

Structuring your message

THIS UNIT LOOKS AT:

■ different ways of structuring e-mail messages, particularly replies

■ useful language for introducing main and supporting points (e.g. *firstly, ...;
as a result of ...*) and for directing the reader (e.g. *please see below*)

Context **Look at the e-mail extracts below showing how different people have replied to
incoming e-mails. Match each e-mail to one or more of these subjects.**

meeting	report	software	results

A

Dear Steve
Thank you for your e-mail. Please see my responses in between your requests
below.
Best wishes
Louis

> Please could you give me the production figures for last August? I need to
send them to head office by the end of the week.
They're on your desk.

> I need to see all the production staff on Thursday. Can you ring around and
arrange a suitable time for everyone, and then book a room?
The meeting will start at 4 p.m. and will take place in the boardroom.

B

Dear Martin

Thank you for your e-mail. Please could you give me a call on extension 343 to
arrange a time when I can come and look at your computer.

Best regards
Janet
- - -Original Message - - -
   From: M. Monroe
    Sent: 28 November 2003 09:45
      To: J. Cooper
 Subject: Computer problems

Dear Janet
Please could you take a look at my computer, which keeps crashing? I think this
is as a result of the new program I've loaded onto it recently to help us keep
track of distribution.

c

Dear Rachel
Thank you for your e-mail of 11th March about the internal monthly production report. A summary of the report can be found below this message. It is divided into three parts:
1 scheduling
2 production
3 distribution

Please could you forward the relevant information to staff in your unit.
Best regards
Joseph Meek

1 Scheduling
New schedules were developed by production working group, as a result of a discussion held between employee representatives and management on 24th February.

Presentation
Structuring e-mails

1 a **Look at the above e-mails again. Which of the ways of structuring e-mails outlined below are used?**

1 Include the whole of the previous e-mail beneath your reply.

2 Quote relevant part(s) of the previous message.

3 Summarize in the first few lines the purpose of the e-mail, and provide additional information below.

4 Keep your message short and provide an attachment (e.g. in Word, Excel, PowerPoint) containing further details.

b **Consider the advantages and disadvantages of each approach.**

2 a **Which of the approaches in Exercise 1 would you use to structure the reply to the e-mail below? Give your reasons.**

To:	[*your e-mail address*]
From:	H.Beam@ibu.com
Subject:	Visitors on 23rd August

Dear [*your name*]

Thank you for agreeing to show the visitors around the plant on 23rd August between 2.30 and 4.30. I would appreciate it if you could let me know which areas you plan to visit so that I can finalise the itinerary.
Please could you also let me know what Health and Safety clothing the visitors will need, if any.

With grateful thanks
Helena Beam

b **Write your reply.**

3 What other factors can ensure that your e-mail is well structured? Compare your ideas with the tips below.

- Reading on screen can sometimes be difficult, so try to keep your e-mail as short as possible. The receiver should not have to scroll down too far to read the whole message.

- Ensure your main points can be found easily. Introduce each one clearly (e.g. *Firstly, ...*).

- Use short paragraphs which are well spaced. Ideally, each paragraph should contain one main idea.

- Direct readers to the relevant part(s) of your message (e.g. *See below ...*).

- Consider numbering or bullet points, using headings and sub-headings, or highlighting key information (e.g. *at 3 p.m.*).

Introducing main/ supporting points

4 Look at the e-mail below sent by Johannes Steiner, BTP's Regional Production Manager in Germany, in reply to an e-mail from Martin Kilsby, European Production Director. What are:

1 the main points?

2 the supporting points, e.g. explanations in support of the main points (*This is due to ...*) and the implications of these (*This will lead to ...*)?

To: m-kilsby@btp.com
From: j-steiner@btp.com
Subject: February production figures

 Attachments:

production_march_12.xls

Dear Mr Kilsby

Please find attached the latest production figures for BTP **Friedrichshafen**, Karlsruhe and Baden, as mentioned in your e-mail of 9th March. I would like to draw three points to your attention in relation to these figures.

Firstly, you will notice that production at Friedrichshafen has risen by more than **25%** compared to the last quarter. This is as a direct result of taking on 75 new production staff at the plant.

Secondly, production rates at the **Karlsruhe** factory were **15%** lower than in the previous quarter. This fall is due to unexpected technical difficulties with the new machinery for the production line. These problems have led to delays of up to twelve hours at a time.

Finally, in response to growing demand for industrial chemicals from the Far East, the **Baden** plant plans to **increase production** from March onwards. This means that the company will need to recruit as many as 100 additional shop-floor staff to cover the extra shifts proposed.

If you have any questions or would like any further information, please do not hesitate to contact me.

Best regards
Johannes Steiner

> I am writing to remind you all that the February production figures are due in by the end of the week.
> Best regards
> Martin Kilsby

---

5 a **Find words and phrases used in the e-mail to introduce:**

Main points	Supporting points
firstly	due to

b **Add any additional words and phrases from the e-mails in the Context section.**

6 Referring back to Exercises 1 and 3 on pages 17 and 18, consider other ways of structuring Johannes Steiner's e-mail effectively.

Directing the reader **7 Look through the e-mails in the unit so far and find phrases used to direct readers to different parts of their message. Add to the list below.**

Directing the reader

See points 3–5 below for more details …

As you can see in the attached …

Paragraph 3 below deals with …

1 Rearrange the words to make the six main points in an e-mail report.

1 the company firstly plans invest to new machinery € 5 million in
2 production have rates increased secondly by 25%
3 there is products growing our thirdly demand for
4 the company decided finally 100 has take to new on staff
5 company's firstly has there a change to the been policy
6 finally product will invested be in $100,000 development

Introducing supporting points

2 Complete these supporting points from an e-mail report.

1 I apologize for the delay in sending this report. This is due to ...
2 We have experienced a number of production problems. This is as a result of ...
3 As agreed, € 500,000 will be invested in new machinery over the next five years, which will mean that ...
4 There's been a recent decision to expand the plant. This will probably lead to ...
5 We have decided to take on 25 new production staff. This is in response to ...
6 Owing to ..., there will be delays to the deliveries to the warehouse.
7 Because of ..., we hope to be able to provide a better service in the future.

3 Complete the gaps in the sentences below using these words.

information	below	between	attached	paragraph	after

1 As stated in your original message _____ , the deadlines are very tight.

2 Please see the suggested production schedule _____ .

3 My responses are in _____ each of the points raised.

4 See _____ 3 below for employees' recommendations.

5 My responses can be found directly _____ each of your questions.

6 See the attached file for further _____ .

4 🎧 2.1 Listen to a voicemail from the Production Manager of BTP's plant in Valencia, Spain. Then write two e-mails:

1 one to the Production Manager confirming that you will do what he requests;

2 one to the staff.

Use the notes below to help you write the e-mails, making sure that they are both well structured.

Main points	Supporting points
1 €50 million expansion to plant	• building three times bigger
	• higher production capacity
	• better facilities
	• improved goods despatch area
2 Six new factories	• at least 150 new jobs
	• wider range of products

Tip Check you have the facts to hand and you can support your main points.

Consolidation

1 **Think of an e-mail you need to write for work.**

2 **Note down your main and supporting ideas in the framework on page 57 of the Resources section.**

3 **Write your e-mail.**

4 **Reflect on what you have written. How clear is the structure of your e-mail?**

➔ NOW TURN TO YOUR LEARNING JOURNAL AND MAKE NOTES ON THIS UNIT.

Reference

Useful phrases

Introducing main ideas

Firstly, ...

Secondly, ...

Thirdly, ...

Finally, ...

Introducing supporting ideas

This is *as a result of* delays installing the new equipment.

Output will be reduced *because of* the industrial action.

This is *due to* difficulties we are experiencing with the machinery

This is *in response to* an increased demand for the new product.

This will probably *lead to* short-term disruption.

This will *mean* that our production capacity will increase.

There will be a short delay in responding *owing to* the postal strike.

Directing the reader

See below for further information.

Figures can be found below.

See paragraph 3 for full details.

Please find attached ...

As you can see in the attached file, ...

Point 4 above deals with ...

My responses can be found directly after each of your questions.

As stated in your original message below, ...

A summary of the report can be found beneath this message.

Vocabulary

Visiting a factory

expand/expansion

facilities

factory

goods dispatch area

health and safety (clothing)

industrial chemicals

install/installation

invest/investment (in machines)

itinerary

machinery

plant

schedules

shift

shop-floor staff

Production

capacity

costs

line

manager

operatives

problems

rates

targets

Study suggestion   Put new words or phrases on cards, with a translation into your own language on the back.

Review

1 How many words can you find in the unit that go with the word *production*?

Example: production manager

2 Put these words in order to make sentences.

1 investment the is higher expected than firstly

2 production our targets than 15% are lower year last secondly

3 as high rates production in Shanghai are as finally those Beijing in

4 production in rise a to in this is response

5 increase changes the will lead to production in an capacity

3 a 🎧 **2.2 Listen to a voicemail message from Martine Burckhardt, BTP's Swiss Regional Production Manager, asking you to send an e-mail on her behalf to Martin Kilsby. Make notes on what you have to include.**

b This is the e-mail you have written. Check it for any factual errors.

To: m-kilsby@btp.com
From: k-beck@btp.com
Subject: Production report

📎 btp_prod_rep.doc

Dear Mr Kilsby

I am attaching the production report for the last quarter, on behalf of Martine Burckhardt. Please note that production rates at the Zürich plant were lower than expected. This is because of problems experienced with the newly installed production equipment.

The rates of production in Geneva are almost the same as those in Lucerne. This is as a direct result of the new staff recruitment policy.

The Basel branch is likely to close by November. This will mean that some production staff will soon be asked to relocate to Lucerne.

If you would like further information about the report, please contact Martine Burckhardt on extension 493859.

Best regards
Kevin Beck

---

4 Look at the following e-mail extract and the notes you took during a presentation. Write the reply, checking that your e-mail is well structured.

- will move production of Model 364 overseas → need to lower production costs
- will invest in website → growing client interest in ordering products via the Internet
- will sell in euros → need to update systems and inform clients

---

I am writing about yesterday's presentation in which Martin Kilsby outlined changes to BTP's future strategy. Unfortunately, no one from the German sites was able to attend.
I would be grateful if you could send me a summary of the issues raised, which I will forward to the other production managers in Baden, Karlsruhe and Friedrichshafen.

Best regards
Luca Joekel

UNIT 3

Being clear and concise

THIS UNIT LOOKS AT:

- factors affecting clarity, such as layout and language
- language for linking ideas (*however ...*), giving examples (*such as ...*) and explaining (*that is to say ...*)

Context **Look at the e-mail extracts below and answer these questions.**

1 In A, is it clear what June is writing about?

2 In B, do we know what is postponed?

3 In C, what do you think are the words missing from the screen?

4 In D, do we know when the interviews are exactly?

5 In E, what jobs are available?

A

> To: P.Schmidt@IGR.com
> From: J.Daws@IGR.com
> Subject:
>
> Dear Peter
> I've got an appointment to see my son's teacher at ten o'clock in the morning – that's up in the centre. I was supposed to go today, but she called me up just as I was about to drive there and said that she would have to postpone it – not sure why, though. Anyway, I'm not likely to be back much before lunchtime, I wouldn't think, so I suggest we meet on * 21st* instead in Room 123 to discuss NECTP23, if the room's available on that day, of course, but if it isn't, we'll have to use another room, possibly on the floor below. Could you perhaps give me a call, or if you prefer you could just send me an e-mail to let me know if you can make it or not.
>
> Cheers,
> June

B

> To: sales@ivt.fi
> From: jari-mikkonen@ivt.fi
> Subject:
>
> Please note that it has been postponed until 4th January.
> Jari

C

> Markus
> you for your help yesterday with processing the applications for the marketing assis

D

> To: alisonjacob@aol.com
> From: mk1@compuserve.com
> Subject: Marketing Officer interviews
>
> Dear Ms Jacob
> I am writing to confirm that you have been shortlisted for the post of Marketing Officer at MK1 Consulting. Interviews will take place next month. I would be grateful if you could confirm that you will be able to attend.
> Yours sincerely
>
> Jackie Price
> Personnel Officer

E

> Dear Mrs Reilly
> Thank you for your e-mail in which you enquired about vacancies at HRT International.
> We are currently recruiting personnel for the following posts:
> • financial advisor
> • clerical assistant
> • legal secretary
> For information on all current vacancies, visit our website:
> http://www.letsgo.com or contact our HR department on 08978 384938.

Presentation
Being clear and concise

I Look at the e-mails on these pages again and consider these questions.

1 How easy or difficult is it to find key information in these e-mails? Give your reasons.

2 What would make it easier for you to find key information?

3 Which of the five e-mails is the clearest in terms of content and layout?

2 Complete the guidelines below with these words and phrases.

> graphics   repetition   subject   paragraphs   sentences
> length   italics   linking   jargon   consistent

Best practice – being clear and concise

1 Keep your e-mail as short as possible to keep scrolling to a minimum. Your message is then more likely to be read.

2 Keep your _____ short and simple (15–20 words maximum).

3 Use short _____ (e.g. four to six sentences), with generous spacing in between.

4 Limit your line _____ to about 65–70 characters.

5 Where possible, use active verb forms to make it clear who needs to do what.

6 Be _____ in your use of key terms to avoid confusion.

7 Give examples or explanations, where appropriate, of _____ and any other language that the reader may not know.

8 Use ___linking___ words like *however* or *and* to organise your ideas.

9 Avoid unnecessary _____ .

10 Use shorter words rather than long phrases where appropriate.

11 Use clear _____ lines – you don't want the receiver to think your mail is spam.

12 Use bold type or _____ to emphasise important points. But remember that formatting and special characters do not always transfer well between different systems. Avoid underlining key points – they look like web links.

13 Avoid sending large _____ or images.

Tip Avoid jargon wherever possible. Remember that the receiver may not be familiar with your area of business.

3 Choose two of the e-mails from these pages. To what extent do they follow the guidelines?

4 Look at these two sentences. Which of the underlined phrases is used to give:

1 an example?

2 an explanation?

a The meeting is in HR2, <u>that is</u>, Room 2 in the Human Resources building.

b I think we should invite a member of the Finance Department to the meeting, <u>for example</u> Claudio.

5 Look at the phrases below. Which are used to give:

1 an example?

2 an explanation?

that is to say	this stands for	this means that	in other words
such as	to give an example	to put it another way	for instance
	for example	that is	

6 What do the following abbreviations and acronyms stand for?

1 i.e.   **2** e.g.   **3** re.   **4** ASAP   **5** Ltd   **6** pp   **7** VAT   **8** PLC

7 Look at these two sentences. How could you shorten the second sentence without the meaning becoming unclear?

Janet suggested we put the job advertisement in *Business Weekly*. Putting the advertisement in *Business Weekly* is a really good idea, I think.

8 a Join a sentence from A and a sentence from C using a word/phrase from B.

A	B	C
1 We are all busy	**but**	my colleague advised me not to.
2 You'll need to complete an application form	**and**	they probably won't take me on.
3 I will put the ad in the local paper	**despite**	the meeting will still go ahead.
4 I applied for a job at RPT International	**although**	I will put it in the national press.
5 I'm going to take the job at Miltons	**However,**	send us your CV.
6 I nearly applied for the sales vacancy	**In addition,**	the poor pay.

b Which of the words or phrases are used to add information? Which are used to contrast information?

c How many more words/phrases can you think of to join the sentences?

Example: also

Practice

*Giving examples/
explanations*

1 **Complete the sentences appropriately.**

Example
Twenty-five people have applied to take part in Project 546FRT, that is, the one on online recruitment.

1 Very few candidates filled in the application correctly. To give an example, ...

2 Unfortunately, the conference room is booked all day Thursday. This means that ...

3 We need to discuss a number of issues during the sales meeting, such as ...

4 There are several reasons why we hold our departmental meetings on Mondays. For instance, ...

5 The applicants for the vacancy all have degrees. To put it another way, ...

6 The meeting's in Block P, which stands for ...

7 There's a lot on the agenda tomorrow, for example ...

*Avoiding repetition/
Using shorter words*

2 **Make these sentences more concise by replacing the phrases in italics with one word only.**

1 There are three items for discussion on today's agenda. The most important *item for discussion* is recruitment.

2 Could you make ten copies of the report for the meeting, please? Could you give *the ten copies of the report* to the participants beforehand?

3 *In the normal course of events*, we hold departmental meetings on the first Tuesday of each month.

4 I don't think we have time to discuss this *at this moment in time*.

5 *In view of the fact that* the meeting room has been double-booked, I suggest we reschedule the meeting for 3rd July.

6 Jonathan suggested that we postpone the meeting for a week. I think *postponing the meeting for a week* would be a good idea.

3 **Cross out any unnecessary words and phrases to shorten this e-mail.**

> The interview's taking place in two months' time – on 21st September,
> actually. Anyway, I'm not worrying about it, not at this moment in time at
> least. They said it'll be in Coventry at a hotel called the Leofric Hotel. It's in the
> city centre, by the way.

Linking words   **4** **Complete the gaps in these sentences using words and phrases from Exercise 8 on page 26.**

1   Only half the staff turned up at the meeting, _____ receiving a reminder the day before.

2   Can you take the minutes for us today, Jane? Could you _____ type them up after the meeting?

3   I'd like to hold the interviews next week. _____ , we need to give candidates more notice, really.

4   I'll send out details of the interviews to the applicants today. _____ , I'll book rooms for the interviews.

5   _____ I'd given participants copies of the agenda before the meeting, no one remembered to bring them.

5 **Rewrite e-mail A on page 24 to make it clearer and more concise.**

6 **Write a clear and concise e-mail to send to your team using the e-mail below and your handwritten notes.**

Office Block 9

> Subject: Work number 308493
>
> Please could you make all of your staff aware of the following information
> below. Please be advised that the following maintenance works will be taking
> place shortly. The power will be down in OB9 in the first week of May for the
> period starting Monday 1st May and ending Wednesday 3rd May. The works are
> expected to last for up to four hours in total overall. In the event that work is
> taking place, most staff who normally work within the building will be affected.
> All daytime visitors to the building will be affected. There are no expected
> health and safety issues. Staff are asked to follow any instructions given while
> this work is being carried out. Smoking will not be allowed while the work is
> being carried out. We apologize for any inconvenience caused.

those who work the nightshift not affected

e.g. interviewees for the Production Operative vacancies

Tip Try not to make your reader scroll down too far. They may miss your key points.

7 **You have agreed to meet your manager to discuss the progress of a project you have been working on. Unfortunately, you will not be able to make the agreed date. Write an e-mail to your manager explaining the situation and suggesting an alternative day to meet. Check your e-mail using the checklist on page 57 of the Resources section.**

8 a Read this e-mail. What do you think the following abbreviations stand for?

1 CV

2 wpm

3 K

4 p.a.

To: all-staff@hv.co.uk
From: p-green@hv.co.uk
Subject: Internal vacancy

From September 7th there will be a vacancy at the Birmingham office for a marketing assistant. The successful applicant will have good communication and secretarial skills (60 wpm).
The starting salary for the post will be £15K p.a.
Interested members of staff should e-mail their CV to Steve Higgins at
s-higgins@hv.co.uk
Best regards
Peter Green

b E-mail Peter Green expressing an interest in the vacancy. Explain why you are applying and give examples of your previous experience.

Consolidation

1 **Think of an e-mail you often need to write for work (e.g. to book a meeting room).**

2 **Write the e-mail.**

3 **Before you send it, check it carefully using the checklist on page 57 of the Resources section.**

4 **Save the text of your e-mail (e.g. as a Word document).**

5 **The next time you have to write the same kind of e-mail, copy and paste it into the body of your e-mail.**

→ NOW TURN TO YOUR LEARNING JOURNAL AND MAKE NOTES ON THIS UNIT.

Reference

Useful phrases

Contrasting ideas

We are all busy, *but* the meeting will still go ahead.

We are all busy. *Nevertheless*, the meeting will still go ahead.

I applied for a job at RPT International, *although* they probably won't take me on.

I applied for a job at RPT International. They probably won't take me on, *though*.

I'm going to take the job at Miltons *despite / in spite of* the poor pay.

I nearly applied for the sales vacancy. *However*, my colleague advised me not to.

Adding ideas

I will put the ad in the local paper. *In addition, / Furthermore,* I will put it in the national press.

You'll need to complete an application form *and* send us your CV.

You'll need to complete an application form. You'll *also* need to send us your CV.

Giving examples

Very few candidates filled in the application correctly. *For example, / For instance, / To give an example,* several forgot to sign the last page!

We need to discuss a number of issues during the sales meeting, *such as* the new sales targets and recruiting new staff.

Explaining

Unfortunately, the conference room is booked all day Thursday. *This means that* we'll have to use the boardroom.

The applicants for the vacancy all have degrees. *To put it another way, / That is, / That is to say, / In other words,* they're all overqualified.

The meeting's in OB9. *That stands for* Office Block 9, by the way.

Vocabulary

Meetings and interviews

attend/cancel (a meeting)

be shortlisted (for an interview)

candidate

fill in / complete (an application form)

Human Resources

hold/postpone (interviews/meetings)

interview (a candidate)

items (for discussion)

make (an appointment)

participant

process (applications)

put (an advert in the paper)

recruit/recruitment

(type up / take) the minutes

take place

vacancy

well-qualified

Abbreviations and acronyms

AOB (any other business)

ASAP (as soon as possible)

CV (curriculum vitae)

e.g. (for example)

etc. (and so on)

i.e. (that is)

K (kilo = one thousand)

Ltd (limited)

PLC (public limited company)

Re. (with reference to)

VAT (value added tax)

p.a. (per annum)

pp (per person / pages)

wpm (words per minute)

Study suggestion   Try to expand your vocabulary by recording words with those which have a similar meaning, e.g. *to take on* = *to recruit*; *plant* = *factory*.

Review

1 Complete the guidelines for being clear using these words.

avoid	give	use	make	keep

1 _____ your sentences short (15–20 words).

2 _____ sure your main points stand out.

3 _____ jargon/abbreviations.

4 _____ examples.

5 _____ linking words.

2 Replace the phrases in italics with one word.

1 The new staff have been at the company for two weeks. *The new staff* seem to have settled in well.

2 We're going to hold the meeting on 23rd November – *the reason is because* everyone is available then.

3 The meeting will take place on 13th February. *The meeting* will probably last just under an hour.

4 I look forward to *meeting up with* you on Friday.

5 We've been having problems finding well-qualified staff. *These kinds of* problems will hopefully be addressed in next month's meeting.

6 We will *make a decision* about the candidates by 10th February.

3 Improve the clarity and conciseness of this e-mail.

> Before you can choose the online course you want to sign up for, you need to register with LearnBusiness.net. If you want to register and you haven't done so already, these are the instructions you need to follow. You can register with LearnBusiness.net in a number of different ways. You will receive a registration card two to three days after you register. Forms are available from our website at http://www.lb.net. You can collect a registration form from your local business forum. Fill in the form in black ink. Once you have done this, sign the registration form and then you can return the form to LearnBusiness.net, 36 Primrose Drive, Masden MT12 9YR. Make sure that you complete a separate course registration form for each of the courses you are applying for. If you would like a full list of business forums, this is available by telephoning the LearnBusiness.net hotline on 0194 3845930. The telephone line is open 9–5.30, seven days a week, Monday to Sunday.

4 Write an e-mail to request an application pack for a job recently advertised in the national press.

5 a 3.1 **Look at the e-mail Pierre Jardin, a new member of staff, has received. What do you think *AM*, *F102* and *A Block* mean? Listen to the conversation Pierre has with a colleague and check your answers.**

> You have been invited to meet the AM tomorrow afternoon. The meeting will take place at two o'clock in F102 in A Block.

b Using the information in the transcript (page 61), rewrite the e-mail to Pierre, making it clearer.

UNIT 4

Choosing the right level of formality

THIS UNIT LOOKS AT:

■ features of formal and informal e-mails

■ factors to consider when choosing the right level of formality

■ useful language for being formal and informal
(*would you mind* …; *thanks for…**)

Context

Levels of formality

I Look at these e-mails. Put them in order from the most formal (1) to the least formal (3).

A

> To: makki.e.rajala@hort.com
> From: LaurenMajor@PTU.co.uk
> Subject: Your latest order
>
> ---
>
> Makki,
> I just wanted to let you know that I got your order today. I'm really sorry, but we've run out of the blue folders. Can you get in touch and let me know whether red ones would be OK instead?
>
> Best wishes
> Lauren

B

> To: johnmartin@marlow.org.uk
> From: Q_Wan@cav.com
> Subject: Hi john
>
> ---
>
> Hi
> Thanks for your order – got it today. Will send off all the stuff to you straight away. Thanks a lot! J
>
> B4N
> Qing

C

> To: m_nathan@nyh.com
> From: j.martin@ahorn.fr
> Subject: Stationery order of 12 August
>
> ---
>
> Dear Mr Nathan
>
> Thank you for your stationery order of 12 August.
>
> I have pleasure in confirming that the goods have been dispatched to you today. If you require any further information, or would like to place another order, please do not hesitate to contact me.
>
> Yours sincerely
> Jean Martin
> Sales Assistant

1 Look at the e-mails on page 32 and answer these questions.

1 What are typical features of (a) informal and (b) formal e-mails?

2 What factors are important to consider when deciding whether to write an informal or formal e-mail?

2 🎧 **4.1 Listen to Catherine Piper, a Communications Manager, and compare your answer to question 2 above.**

Guidelines **3 Look at the three extracts below taken from company guidelines. Match each extract with one of the e-mails on page 32.**

1

> You should always use an informal style in all e-mails to appear friendly and approachable. This means that you can start an e-mail with *Hi/Dear* and end *Best regards*. You may also use contractions (*don't*, etc). Avoid passive forms where possible (*It has been said ...*, etc).

2

> An e-mail can be read and forwarded to anyone in the world, so make sure yours leaves a positive impression, both of you and the company. If you wouldn't say it in a letter, don't say it in your e-mail.

3

> Although it's safer to be more rather than less formal, especially in external e-mails, there are no hard-and-fast rules. Be guided by the other person. If they use an informal style to you, it's acceptable for you to use a similar style when responding. However, use Internet abbreviations (CU, etc.) and emoticons (:-(etc.) in informal internal e-mails only.

Tip Passives are often used in more formal e-mails.

4 Does your company have any guidelines for the level of formality you should use in internal and external e-mails? If so, what do they say? If not, what would you include in them?

5 Find phrases in the e-mails on page 32 to add to the table below.

	Formal	Informal
A Thanking someone	*Thank you very much for ...* *Thank you for ...*	
B Asking someone to do something	*Would you mind ...?*	*Can you ...?*
C Confirming something	*I wish to confirm ...*	*I just wanted to let you know ...*
D Apologizing for	*I would like to apologize for ...* *I apologize for ...*	

6 Find words in the e-mails on page 32 to do with 'orders and supplies'. Put them in the table below. Use your dictionary to help you.

Formal	Informal
	stuff

7 What different ways can you think of to begin and end formal and informal e-mails? Give examples of when you have used each of these and why. (Look at the e-mails in this unit and in Unit 1 for examples.)

8 What do these informal Internet abbreviations stand for?

1 2L8   2 AFAIK   3 IOW   4 TIA   5 B4N   6 CU   7 CUL   8 OTOH   9 TKS
10 FYI   11 BTW   12 FAQs

Practice

Formal language

1 Replace the phrases in italics using a more formal phrase.

Example: *I'm happy to say* that your order has been dispatched.

I have pleasure in confirming that your order has been dispatched.

1 *I just wanted to let you know* that your order has been processed.
2 *Can* I place an order by phone, please?
3 *I'm really sorry about* the delay to your order.
4 *Thanks* for your order.
5 *Can* you confirm your contact details, please?

Informal language

2 Complete these sentences using the most informal word or phrase in brackets.

Example: I hope you found the service (~~satisfactory~~ / OK).

1 I ('m really sorry / apologize for) the delay.
2 Thanks (a lot / very much) for all your help.
3 I (got / received) your order form this morning – many thanks!
4 Can you (contact / get in touch with) Janet asap?
5 This is just to (let you know / inform you) that the (stuff / goods) arrived OK.

A received order

3 Put these sentences in the correct order to create an e-mail about a received order.

a   Margaret Nelmes (Customer Services Manager)

b   Thank you for placing an order with BFT Direct.

c   Your order is now being processed.

d   Subject: Order No. 556454

e   Once we have received the goods from our suppliers, you will be contacted to arrange a convenient delivery date.

f   Dear Miss Beech

g   Alternatively, call our customer services division on 08939 385030.

h   Yours sincerely,

i   Meanwhile, if you wish to contact us regarding your order, please e-mail us on: bft_orders@bft.com

4 Rewrite these sentences using the prompts to make them more formal.

Example: I've put a copy of our latest brochure in the post to you today. (A copy of …)

A copy of our latest brochure has been put in the post to you today.

1 Can you let me have some more details of the discounts you offer? (We would appreciate …)

2 I place a stationery order once a month. (A stationery order …)

3 I'll cancel the order as soon as I can. (The order …)

4 I'm sorry about any problems this may cause. (We apologize …)

5 Write a short e-mail to a colleague you know well thanking them for helping you to process some orders and asking for their help in the future.

6 a 4.2 **You work for a supplier of computer hardware. Listen to a voicemail message from a customer who has not received an order. As you listen, make notes below.**

Name:

Company:

Order no:

Order details:

b Write an e-mail in reply.

Tip As you write, consider the level of formality that your reader expects.

7 Some of the following lines have extra words in them. Find the extra words and write them in the space on the right of the e-mail. If a line is correct put a tick (✔).

> To: Hugo.Grant@tria.fi
> From: G.Hellios@millino.com
> Subject: Missing order
>
> Dear Mr Grant
>
> I am sorry to hear about the problems you   1 _____
>
> have been experienced with the order   2 _been_____
>
> you did placed with us on 23rd June.   3 _did_____
>
> I cannot yet to say who is at fault but I assure   4 _to_____
>
> you there will be a most full investigation.   5 _there/most_____
>
> Jessie Black, who our production assistant,   6 _who_____
>
> will contact you shortly to arrange suitable   7 _____✔_____
>
> compensation for the many inconvenience   8 _many_____
>
> that you have been caused.   9 _____✔_____
>
> I would like to apologise once more again.   10 _more_____
>
> Yours very sincerely   11 _very_____
>
> Giorgio Hellios

8 Look at the e-mail below. How consistent is the level of formality? What would you change to make the e-mail more consistent?

> Dear Mr Lambert
> Thanks a lot for delivering our recent order for 34 lamps (model 2011) so promptly. We would like to place a follow-up order for 45 of the same model. Give me a call, will you, to discuss discounts for multiple orders.
> TIA
> Barbara Frank

Consolidation

1 Think of an e-mail you need to write for work. Prepare your e-mail using the framework on page 58 of the Resources section.

2 Write the e-mail.

Tip Be consistent in the level of formality you use.

3 Review the e-mail you have written. Is the level of formality appropriate? Have you used this level of formality consistently?

➡ NOW TURN TO YOUR LEARNING JOURNAL AND MAKE NOTES ON THIS UNIT.

Thanking someone

Thank you very much for (your reply).

Thank you for (your e-mail).

Thanks for (your order).*

Thanks a lot (for everything).*

Asking someone to do something

Would you mind phoning the suppliers?

Could you confirm your contact details?

Can you get in touch about your recent order?*

Confirming something

I have pleasure in confirming (that the goods have been dispatched).

I wish to confirm (that I have received your order).

I just wanted to let you know (that I got the stuff).*

Apologizing for something

Please accept my apologies for (the service you have received).

I would like to apologize for (the delay).

I apologize for (the problems you have had).

I'm really sorry, but (we've run out of folders).*

Orders and supplies

cancel/place/process/receive/confirm (an order)

client

contact

customer

customer services

delivery (date/terms)

discount

dispatch

get in touch*

goods

letter of complaint

order

run (out of)*

service

stationery

stuff*

suppliers

Message abbreviations *

2L8	too late
AFAIK	as far as I know
B4N	bye for now
BTW	by the way
CU	see you
CUL	see you later
FAQs	frequently asked questions
FYI	for your information
IOW	in other words
OTOH	on the other hand
TIA	thanks in advance
TKS	thanks

* informal

Review

1 Put the words into the correct order to make standard phrases for use in ordering and dealing with suppliers.

1 I forward look receiving to order your

2 further like would if you any information please do not contact hesitate to me

3 price included VAT is in the

4 we for apologize inconvenience any caused

5 pleasure have I confirming in your that order been has dispatched

6 attaching a I am copy of updated our price list

7 I know just to let wanted I've sent you the order

8 you get can in soon touch as as possible

2 Find the pairs of words or phrases from the e-mails on page 32. Then decide which is the formal and which the informal word or phrase in each pair.

to send   satisfactory   to contact   very much   to get in touch   OK   to regret   stuff   to be sorry   goods   a lot   to need   to require   to get   to dispatch   to receive

3 4.3 Listen to John Martin speaking to a colleague about an e-mail he received from his suppliers (e-mail B on page 32). Then rewrite the e-mail using an appropriate level of formality.

4 Write a short e-mail to a client apologizing for sending the wrong order and confirming the delivery terms for the correct order.

Study suggestion	Keep a record of useful informal expressions, together with their more formal version, e.g. *to get in touch with someone = to contact someone* *to let someone know = to tell someone* Also, as you record new words and phrases, note whether they are formal (f.) or informal (inf.), e.g. *stuff* (inf.); *to regret* (f.); *a lot of* (inf.); *goods* (f.)

UNIT 5

Getting the tone right

THIS UNIT LOOKS AT:

■ the importance of making a good impression on the recipient

■ useful language for being polite (*Shall I …; of course you can …*)

■ ways of altering the tone of your message (*highly …; quite…*)

Context
Responses

1 **Match each e-mail 1–3 with a response A–C.**

1

> Would you mind if I took 13th July off work? I'd really like to attend a sales conference in Brighton.
> Regards

2

> I've got some free time this afternoon. Would you like me to help you to arrange your business trip to Paris?
> Best wishes

3

> I've booked your hotel accommodation for next week, as requested. I'm attaching details of the arrangements. Please could you confirm you are happy with them.
> Thank you

A

> It looks like you have made a mistake. I asked for a room with a shower, not a bath. Sort it out as soon as you can, will you.

B

> NO, YOU CAN'T. WE'RE FAR TOO BUSY THEN.

C

> I don't really need any help. I can manage just fine on my own!

2 a How would you feel if you received each of the responses on page 40? Choose an emoticon. Give your reasons.

the responses on page 40?

:-)   :)   :-(;-)   :-0   :->   :/   :-D

b 🎧 5.1 Listen to what the recipients said about the e-mails.

Presentation
Tone

1 Think of two e-mails you have received recently. Which of these adjectives would you use to describe each of them? Which do you think the recipients would use to describe two e-mails you sent recently?

> friendly   abrupt   sarcastic   direct   tentative   polite   confident
> jokey   rude   positive   professional

2 How easy do you find it to write short, quick business e-mails without being too direct, or appearing rude or aggressive?

Policy

3 Complete the gaps in the following extract from an e-mail policy using the phrases in the box. Brainstorm other ways of completing the gaps in the extracts.

> anyone throughout the world
>
> between colleagues
>
> you are shouting
>
> any body language
>
> your purpose
>
> get someone to check your e-mail first
>
> sensitive

1 Respond fully to all external e-mails within four hours. (Where this is impossible, and to avoid rushing off an e-mail that may cause offence, send a short message to let the person know when to expect a full response from you.)

2 Think carefully about what you write. Your e-mail is a permanent record and can be forwarded to _____ .

3 Be careful of your tone. Unlike with other communication (face-to-face, telephone, etc.), there is not _____ .

4 Adapt your tone to suit the relationship you have with the reader and _____ .

5 Don't write the whole message in capital letters. It gives the impression that _____ .

6 Don't send an angry e-mail ('flaming'). It's better to _____ .

7 You may use smileys, emoticons, etc. (:)), but only _____ .

8 Consider whether e-mail is the most appropriate method of communicating your message. For example, avoid using e-mail for situations which are _____ – have a face-to-face meeting or use the telephone instead.

4 a Look at these phrases from the e-mails in this unit.

1 Would you mind if I took 13th July off work?

2 Would you like me to help you to arrange your business trip to Paris?

3 Please could you confirm you are happy with the arrangements.

Which phrase is used to:

A offer to do something?

B ask someone to do something?

C ask to be allowed to do something?

b Now look at the phrases below and decide which category (A, B or C) each belongs in.

1 Would you cancel my hotel reservation for me?

2 Do you mind if I make a change to my booking?

3 Shall I arrange for a taxi to pick us up from the airport?

4 I would be grateful if you could send the invoice directly to me.

5 Can you organise my transfers, please?

6 May I amend my hotel arrangements?

7 Let me meet you at the airport.

8 Would you mind calling the conference centre to confirm our arrival time?

9 I could meet you at the station if you like.

10 Would it be possible to change the time of my flight?

5 Which sentence in each pair is the most direct?

1 a Sort out the arrangements for me, will you?

   b Please could you sort out the arrangements for me?

2 a I need you to help me with the report.

   b Would you mind helping me with the report?

Tip Don't be upset by e-mails that appear to be rude. Some cultures are just more direct than others.

6 What do these changes do to the strength of the writer's message?

1 It's a bad idea. ➜ It's **not a very** good idea.

2 The airport is modern. ➜ The airport is **fairly** modern.

3 I'll pick you up at 9 a.m. ➜ I **might** pick you up at 9 a.m.

4 I recommend the Hotel Bristol. ➜ I **highly** recommend the Hotel Bristol.

5 My colleague's meeting me for lunch. ➜ My colleague's **probably** meeting me for lunch.

6 It's inconvenient. ➜ It's **not very** convenient.

7 I agree with your plans. ➜ I **completely** agree with your plans.

8 You should leave at 7 a.m. ➜ You **must** leave at 7 a.m.

Practice
Polite alternatives

1 Rewrite the sentences below to make them less direct using the prompts.

1 I want a single room with an ensuite bathroom. (Could …)

2 Send me your latest hotel brochure. (Would you …)

3 I need a taxi to pick me up from the airport at 10.30 on Monday. (Can you …)

4 Cancel my flight, will you. (Would you mind …)

5 Leave us your contact details for Paris before you leave. (Would you …)

6 You haven't paid your hotel bill. (The hotel bill doesn't seem …)

7 I want a room with a view. (Would it be possible …)

8 Confirm my reservation by faxing me on 00 43 485 39489. (I would be grateful if …)

Tip Consider whether a reader would find your own e-mails rude or too demanding.

Altering the tone

2 Complete the sentences below using one of the words in the box.

highly	really	quite	entirely	much	definitely	far	very

1 I disagree _____ with what you said earlier about the conference.

2 The hotel's not _____ good.

3 The hotel was _____ better than I expected.

4 I _____ recommend the Hilton Hotel in Budapest.

5 The trip was _____ nice, I suppose, but not wonderful.

6 The course in Paris wasn't _____ that useful.

7 I'd _____ rather you didn't take Tuesday off.

8 I'd _____ go to Prague again.

Giving rules

3 What would you tell a new employee joining your company? Complete the prompts.

1 Everyone here must …

2 People should …

3 We can …

4 You might like to …

5 We could …

Polite responses

4 Match each question with a short but polite response.

1 May I take part in the e-learning training course in Geneva?

2 Do you mind if we have the sales conference on 13th July rather than 7th? It'll mean staff from the Munich branch can also attend.

3 Would you mind if I took a day off work next week to attend part of the project management conference in Berlin?

4 Shall I meet the visitors at their hotel tomorrow?

5 Would you like me to phone for a taxi to take the visitors back to the airport tomorrow evening?

6 Would you like me to book your flight and make a hotel reservation for your business trip to Helsinki?

a Thanks for asking, but Shelly's already called.

b It's very kind of you to offer, but Mark has already agreed to pick them up.

c Thank you for your offer. It would be really helpful if you could organize everything for me.

d By all means postpone the event for a week. It sounds like a very good idea.

e Of course you can attend. Just let me know when this will be.

f I'd rather you didn't take Tuesday off, but any other day would be fine.

Tip Get someone to check the tone of your e-mail before you send it or reread it yourself.

5 How would you make each of the responses on page 40 more polite?

6 🎧 **5.2 Listen to a voicemail from a member of your team and write the short e-mail as requested.**

7 Write complete sentences using these prompts.

1 I / pick / up / clients / you / like.

2 you / cancel / my / hotel / reservation / me?

3 possible / change / my / flight?

4 mind / help / me / report?

5 I / rather / you / not / take / holiday / now.

8 Rearrange these sentences to create two separate e-mails. Then decide how you would reply to each one.

a   I've got to go into town after work.

b   Please could you confirm that you have received it.

c   Yours sincerely

d   Pat Griffiths

e   I could take you to the train station at the same time if you like.

f   Dear Franz

g   Subject: Lift to the station

h   Just let me know.

i   Lauren

j   Subject: Accommodation guide

k   Dear Mr Williams

l   I have posted a copy of 'Corporate Accommodation' today.

m   Best wishes

Consolidation   1   **Think of an e-mail you need to write for work.**

Tip Think about what you want to achieve – and use the appropriate strength of tone.

2   **Choose three polite phrases from this unit to use in your e-mail.**

1 _____

2 _____

3 _____

3   **Tick each phrase off as you use it.**

4   **Ask someone to read the e-mail you have written. What adjectives would you use to describe the tone?**

➔ NOW TURN TO YOUR LEARNING JOURNAL AND MAKE NOTES ON THIS UNIT.

Asking to be allowed to do something (and responding)

May I (alter my hotel arrangements)?

Would it be possible to (change my flight time)?

Do you mind if I (pay later)?

Would you mind if I (took 13th July off)?

....

By all means (postpone the event).

Of course you can (attend the session).

I'd rather you didn't (take Tuesday off).

I'm afraid you can't (have the whole day off).

Asking someone to do something

Would/Could/Can* you (cancel my reservation)?

I would be grateful if you could (confirm the time).

Please could you (organize my transfer)?

Would you mind (calling the conference centre)?

Offering to do something (and responding)

Shall I (order a taxi)?

Let me (meet you at the airport).

I could (meet you at the station) if you like.

Would you like me to (help you)?

....

Thanks for asking, but (she's already called).*

It's very kind of you to offer, but (someone has already done it).

Thank you for your offer.

Vocabulary

Business travel

arrange/arrangement

arrival time

attend (a conference)

bill

book (accommodation)

business trip

cancel/change/make/confirm (a reservation)

conference

flight

make (a mistake)

organize (a transfer)

phone (for a taxi)

pick (someone up)

single/double room (with an ensuite bath/shower/view)

sort out (a problem)

Smileys/emoticons

:-) = happy

:) = smiling

:-(= sad/frowning

;-) = winking/flirting/joking

:-O = shocked

:-> = sarcastic

:-/ = thinking

:-D = laughing

---

* informal

Study suggestion   Keep a record of useful prepositional phrases, e.g.
to take part in (a course); to pick someone up (from the station); to take a day off (work)
Also note down useful word partnerships, e.g.
to attend (a conference); to book (accommodation); to cancel (a reservation); to arrange (a trip)

I **Put the words in these questions into the correct order.**

1 call to like would you me taxi a

2 could the you confirm time your of arrival

3 a you mind I later would if took later flight

4 guide to like I'd to speak the tour

5 reference have I may your booking please

6 I the hotel shall book accommodation

2 **Put these phrases in order, from the most to the least polite.**

Is it OK if I ...?   May I ...?   Could I ...?   I want to ...

3 **Make the e-mail below less direct.**

Dear Bernd

I need a return ticket to Frankfurt on 18th August. Send it to my home
address, will you – by Friday if you can.

Hari

4 **Complete the gaps in the e-mail.**

Dear Merle

I'm going to Paris on a business ¹ t_____ from 13th–16th July. I would be
grateful if you could book my ² f_____ and organize ³ a_____ for me. If
possible, I would like a ⁴ s_____ room with an ⁵ e_____ bathroom.

Thank you
Jens

5 **How many more words in the unit can you find to do with business travel?**
Complete the table below.

Noun	Verb	Adjective

6 **You are going on a business trip to Paris. Write an e-mail to the HGF Hotel**
to make a booking. Use the handwritten notes you have made.

- ensuite single room
- river view
- transfer from airport to hotel

Checking before you send

THIS UNIT LOOKS AT:

■ **the importance of accuracy in your writing**

■ **strategies for avoiding careless mistakes**

■ **typical grammar, vocabulary, spelling and punctuation mistakes** (*since/for*; **present simple/continuous;** *make/do*, etc.)

Context   **Look at these e-mail extracts about forthcoming training courses. What initial**
Example e-mails   **impression does each one make on you the reader? Give your reasons.**

A

> To: Janis.Parsons@comp.com
> From: W.Smith@43HU.co.uk
> Subject: Training materials   📎 Training_materials.doc
>
> I have sended you a list of what the materials you must to bring to a training session.

B

> To: Joan.Alexander@crete.fr
> From: Simon.Williams@crete.fr
> Subject: Sales training date
>
> Please note that the postponed sales training will now be held on Thursday 13th February, in Room 314. I would be grateful if you could let me know as soon as possible if you can attend.

But 13th is a Friday!

C

> To: M.Singh@drt.fi
> From: Jon.Smart@men.com
> Subject: Conference
>
> Dear Matti
> Thanking to you for brochur. I like assist conference.

D

> To: P.Dawson@trainuk.com
> From: S.Bass@internetuk.net
> Subject: Training UK conference
>
> I am writing to accept your invitation to give the opening speech at the 'Training UK' conference on 24th July of this year. The title of my speech will be 'e-publishing/e-learning' and will last approximately one hour.

1 a 🎧 6.1 **Listen to this telephone call.**

1 Who is making the call?

2 What is the call about?

3 What will be e-mailed to the caller?

b **Check your answers in the transcript on page 63.**

2 **Look at the documents below. Does the caller receive what was promised? What might he need to clarify with the organizers?**

> Thank you for registering for the 'Online Training for Business' conference, what is taking place in Paris from 7–10 Octobre.
> I have attached the final conference program for Friday as you did request please not that there are any last-minute amendments to the itinery for Wensday and Thursday but there are a little for Friday.
> On Friday, the plenary start at eleven o'clock and will be in Room 311. The workshop in 13:30 has been cancelled, as the principle speaker is ill.

Online Training for Business
8–10 October, Hotel Grand, Paris

Friday 10th October
10:00   Plenary (Room 311)
11:00   Workshop (Room 523) – 'Recent developments in e-learning'
12:00–13:00 Lunch
13:00–14:00 Workshop (Room 546) – 'Research into electronic conferencing'
14:00–14:30 Coffee
14.30–15:30 Free

Conference 3 **Look again at the e-mail in Exercise 2. How accurate is (a) the information and (b) the language? Find examples of grammar, spelling and punctuation errors in the e-mail.**

4 Look at the extracts below from company guidelines.

1 How well did the e-mail writer in Exercise 2 follow what is suggested?

2 Why do you think accuracy of language and information is important in business e-mails?

3 Do you follow these guidelines?

1

Reread the e-mail carefully, or get someone else to read it, to check you've told the recipient everything he/she needs to know – and you've got your facts right. If a meeting's on 14th and you write 13th, the recipient's going to turn up on the wrong day.

2

Check for typing and punctuation errors. An e-mail full of such errors can make a bad impression on the most patient reader – and can even lead to misunderstandings. If it's important enough to send, make sure the reader understands your message!

3

Any writer can make mistakes – but it's important to try and limit these. Before you send your e-mail, use the spell/grammar check. Alternatively, use your dictionary and/or a grammar book to check anything you are not sure of. Phone or send an e-mail to check anything you do not understand.

Tip Spell-checking can help, but doesn't pick up the differences between **its** and **it's**, for example.

Practice
Information

1 a 🎧 6.2 **Listen to a conversation about a training event and make notes below.**

Event:
Date:
Time:

b Check your answers in the transcript on page 64.

2 Now read the e-mail below and correct any information mistakes.

Hi Diane
This is just a quick e-mail to let you know about the sales training event. Mike's just told me it's now going to be on 16th March, not 13th April – I think it's a Tuesday. It starts about eleven and will go on until about five.
Best wishes
Leigh

Tip Be precise about times, dates, etc.

3 Look at these easily confused words. What is the difference between the words in each pair? Check your answers in your dictionary. What other words do you tend to confuse?

Example advice/advise ➜ advice = noun; advise = verb

1 principle/principal

2 interesting/interested

3 personal/personnel

4 valuable/expensive

5 eventually/finally

6 become/receive

7 trainer/trainee

8 however/although

4 Use words from Exercise 3 to complete the gaps in this e-mail.

I hope you've all had a good week.

I'm sorry to announce that we will shortly be losing Val Smith, who has been a very ¹ _____ member of the ² _____ department for over two years now. ³ _____ , Val won't be moving far; she starts her new job at Renoy Communications in the High Street on 21st June. We wish her all the best in her new role as senior ⁴ _____ .

⁵ _____ , I have just ⁶ _____ this week's edition of *Business Leader*. If anyone is ⁷ _____ in borrowing it, just let me know.

Thank you all for your hard work this week. Have a great weekend!

Surjit

5 Does your company prefer you to use American or British spelling? Which word in each pair is American or British English spelling? Check your answers in your dictionary.

1 canceled/cancelled

2 centre/center

3 color/colour

4 organise/organize

5 license/licence

6 practice/practise

7 traveler/traveller

8 labour/labor

9 theater/theatre

Tips

• Whether you use American or British English spelling, be sure you are consistent. If you set your spell-check to British English spelling, it'll highlight American English spelling as errors.

• Note that many people now accept **-ize** spellings in British English, too. However, some words, such as **advertise**, are always spelt **-ise**, even in American English. You just have to learn them!

6 **Remind yourself of the main punctuation uses by looking at the example sentences in the Reference section on page 54. Which of the uses are illustrated in the e-mail in Exercise 4 above? Now punctuate the e-mail extract below appropriately.**

> there are three parts to the course finance marketing and HR Mark Draper will be the main trainer for the finance and marketing sessions Joy Marlow will be responsible for HR do you have any questions about the course content

7 **Look at some typical grammar mistakes. Correct each one. What features of English grammar do you find difficult? Keep a record in the framework on page 58 of the Resources section of your typical mistakes.**

Wrong version	Correct version
1 I have lived here since two years.	
2 If I would have more time, I would take a course.	
3 I am thinking that we should postpone the next training course.	
4 We haven't had much participants on the courses.	
5 The trainer made his best to motivate all the participants.	
6 We all look forward seeing you soon.	
7 There's been a significantly increase in the course cost.	

Tip It's important to be able to identify your language weaknesses. This is the first step in being able to deal with them.

8 **Now complete these sentences appropriately.**

1 At the last conference, there weren't very many ...

2 At work yesterday, I did my best to ...

3 If I had more money, ...

4 I have worked at the same company since ...

5 I think that all training courses ...

6 I look forward ...

7 I've seen a significant ...

9 **Look at the e-mail below. There are some things the writer is not sure about and needs to check before sending the e-mail. Which option would you choose?**

> Dear Mr Chatha
> I [1] *write / am writing* to invite you to [2] *take / have* part in a forthcoming business seminar, [3] *which / what* is due to be held [4] *at / on* 6th June in the Grand Hotel, Altwood. The seminar is entitled '[5] *Doing / Making* Business Online'. Full details of the programme are attached.
> If you [6] *have / will have* any questions or would like any [7] *advise / advice*, please do not hesitate [8] *to contact / contacting* me.
> I look forward to [9] *hearing / hear* from you.
> Yours [10] *faithfully / sincerely*
> Maxine Laportaire

10 **Look at the underlined mistakes the writer has made. How would you correct them? Write the correct word or words in the spaces on the right of the e-mail.**

Dear John	
Thank you for your e-mail about lunch next Thursday.	0 _to meet_
I'd love meeting[0] you, but unfortunately I will attend[1]	1 _____
a course that morning and its[2] not due to finish until	2 _____
2 p.m. If you will be[3] free on Friday, shall we to meet up[4]	3 _____
then? I suggest to go to[5] Starley's. It's a new restaurant	4 _____
which has only been open since[6] four weeks. If you	5 _____
will like,[7] I could do[8] a reservation.	6 _____
Anyway, just let me know.	7 _____
Best wishes	8 _____
Mario	

11 **Improve the e-mail in Exercise 2 of the Presentation section (page 49), correcting the factual as well as the language errors.**

12 a 6.3 **Listen to a voicemail that you have received from a colleague. As you listen, complete your notes below.**

To do
E-mail … about the ….
Date: …
Time: …
Place: …

b **Write the e-mail.**

Consolidation

1 **Prepare a typical e-mail you would need to write for work.**

2 **When you have finished writing it, check it carefully for any mistakes.**

3 **Ask your teacher (or a colleague or friend) to identify the different types of mistakes you have made. Then try to correct them yourself.**

4 **Keep a record of the mistakes you have made.**

5 **If you have worked through Units 1–5 already:**
   a **check your e-mail using the checklist on page 58 of the Resources section;**
   b **draft your own set of 'Best practice' e-mailing guidelines for staff in your company to follow.**

➜ NOW TURN TO YOUR LEARNING JOURNAL AND MAKE NOTES ON THIS UNIT.

Reference *Grammar*

Conditionals

First conditional: *If* + present simple, *will/could/might* + infinitive

If I see him, I will tell him.

Second conditional: *If* + past simple, *would/could/might* + infinitive

If I had more time, I would take a course.

Relatives

The man *that* I was speaking to yesterday is the Production Manager.

Jackie Morgan, *who* is the Media Account Manager, has been promoted.

Do you know *whose* journal that is?

Tomorrow's meeting, *which* starts at ten, will be held in Room 495.

For/since

I have lived here *for* two years/*since* 2001.

Some/any

There are *some* amendments.

There aren't *any* problems.

In/on/at/–

in February / *on* Saturday / *at* the weekend / next week

Much/many

We haven't had *much* success with the course.

There weren't *many* participants.

Gerund/infinitive

I look forward to *hearing* from you.

If you have any questions, please do not hesitate *to contact* me.

Adjectives/adverbs

There's been a *significant* increase in the course cost.

The course cost has increased *significantly*.

Punctuation

Two people are leading the session: Juan and José.

Marco will give Thursday's plenary; Regina will give it on Friday.

The rooms we'll be using are 102, 232, 356, 411 and 455.

The training course was great!

Are you attending the conference, too?

Michaela, who is my boss, is running the course.

Vocabulary

British and American spellings

cancelled/canceled

centre/center

colour/color

labour/labor

licence/license

organise/organize

practise/practice

programme/program

theatre/theater

traveller/traveler

Easily confused words

advise/advice

become/receive

finally/eventually

however/although

interested/interesting

personal/personnel

principal/principle

trainer/trainee

valuable/expensive

Training

course (materials)

give (the plenary / the opening speech)

make (a reservation / a mistake / a plan)

participate/participant

session

train/trainee/trainer/training

workshop

1 Complete the sentences appropriately.

1 I have worked as a trainer for …

2 I don't attend many …

3 Next Wednesday, I …

4 If I had more money, …

5 I look forward to …

6 Do you know whose … ?

7 Please don't hesitate to …

8 We haven't had any …

2 Match the pairs.

1	to take	a	an invitation
2	to accept	b	a course
3	to make	c	a reservation
4	to check	d	business
5	to do	e	a mistake
6	to correct	f	advice
7	to give	g	a record
8	to keep	h	an e-mail

3 Complete the gaps in the sentences using the correct options.

1 *Although / However* the interview wasn't until 4 p.m., I arrived at 3 p.m.

2 Jan Larsson, *who / what* has worked here for three years, is leaving next week.

3 I'm looking forward to *see / seeing* Martina on Wednesday.

4 Is anyone *interested / interesting* in taking the e-learning course?

5 Frances has got an interview this week – I think *its / it's* for the Project Manager job.

6 There haven't been *much / many* applications for the vacancy so far.

4 Find and correct the mistakes in this e-mail extract.

Thank you for your e-mail invitting me to be your plenary speaker at the 'Sales Direct' conference in London in next month. I would be delightful to accept your invitation. However, I am very grateful if you could let me know as soon like possible when exactly the conference is taking place in which centre and what I should speak about.

Study suggestion   Use your dictionary to check for British and American English spellings (e.g. *BrE, AmE*). Also use your dictionary to find word partnerships, i.e. words that go together.

do /duː/ *v.* ~ business, a deal

make /meɪk/ *v.* ~ a suggestion, a decision

Resources

Note: The material on pages 56–58 may be photocopied for use in class.

1 Match the pairs.

1 dot	a	j
2 lower-case j	b	@
3 backslash	c	.
4 colon	d	:
5 forward slash	e	_
6 upper-case j	f	\
7 at	g	/
8 hyphen	h	J
9 underscore	i	-

2 ⌂ 1.1 Listen to the voicemail extracts and complete the table.

E-mail recipient	E-mail address
1	
2	
3	

3 With a partner, take it in turns to dictate e-mail addresses and recipients for each other to write down.

Consider	Notes
Why are you writing?	
Who are you writing to?	
Do you need to cc anyone else into the e-mail?	
What would be a helpful and appropriate subject line?	
Do you need to send an attachment?	
What phrases are you going to use to begin and end your e-mail/refer to previous and future context?	
What do you want the recipient to do when he/she receives the e-mail?	

from *E-mailing* by Louise Pile © DELTA PUBLISHING 2004

Unit 2
Your points

Main points	Supporting points

Useful words and phrases

Unit 3
Checklist

Checklist	Yes/No	Notes
Do the main points stand out (e.g. use of bullets)?		
Is the e-mail written simply and clearly?		
Is the e-mail of a suitable length (i.e. not too long)?		
Are only essential information and words/phrases included (e.g. avoiding phrases like *at this point in time*)?		
Are the sentences of an appropriate length (maximum 20–25 words) and not too full of ideas?		
Have jargon/abbreviations that the reader may not know been explained?		
Are points illustrated/explained clearly, where appropriate (e.g. *such as, that is to say*)?		
Are ideas clearly linked (e.g. *however, and*)?		
Does the subject line clearly show what the e-mail is about?		

Unit 4
Factors to consider

Consider these and other factors	Notes
Your target reader	
Your reason for writing	
Appropriate level of formality	
Useful words/phrases/grammar	

Unit 6
Typical errors

Wrong version	Correct version

Unit 6
Checklist

	Yes/No
Is the purpose clear?	
Is it well structured?	
Is it clear and concise?	
Is the level of formality appropriate?	
Is the tone appropriate?	
Is the language/content accurate?	

from *E-mailing* by Louise Pile © DELTA PUBLISHING 2004

Transcripts and answer keys

Unit 1

Transcripts

1.1
1   Mary, Shelley Aldridge here. I'm going to be late in. Could you e-mail Martin Brown for me and tell him I'll be late for the sales meeting? His e-mail address is m.d.brown24@aol.com.
2   This is Andrew Reilly, that's R-E-I-DOUBLE L-Y, calling about the sales vacancy. Please could you e-mail an application form to A_Reilly – that's capital A, capital R – @bfk.org.uk. Thanks.
3   Katrin, it's Albert. Please could you e-mail me the agenda for tomorrow's meeting? My new e-mail address is a-wyss – that's W-Y-DOUBLE S by the way – @vipon – V-I-P-O-N – .de

1.2
Hi, it's Mary here. Look, do you think you could let Martin know I'm not going to be able to make the marketing seminar today after all? Could you also ask him to ring me afterwards on my mobile? He's got the number. Oh, and perhaps you could copy Katie into the e-mail. Thanks – and see you later.

Answer key

Context
1   1   Sender: Stacey Griffin; Receiver: P. Vogel
    2   Signature: yes   Disclaimer: yes
    3   Yes: 'Sales Manager post (ref. 7672P)'
    4   No
    5   No
    6   To ask whether Mr Vogel would like the application form electronically or in hard copy.
    7   A Word XP document, file size 55K.
    8   Confirm which format he would like.

Presentation
1   1 receiver/recipient   2 cc field   3 signature
    4 disclaimer   5 subject line   7 attachment
    8 To/Cc   9 importance option
3   1   1 c   2 a   3 f   4 d   5 g   6 h   7 b   8 i   9 e
    2

E-mail recipient	E-mail address
1 Martin Brown	m.d.brown24@aol.com
2 Andrew Reilly	A_Reilly@bfk.org.uk
3 Albert Wyss	a-wyss@vipon.de

5   See Reference section on page 14.
6   1 a   2 c   3 f   4 d   5 b   6 e
8   1 b   2 d   3 c   4 a

The phrases you use will depend on factors such as company policy and who you're e-mailing (see Unit 4). When e-mailing friends, you might use *Hi / Bye for now*. When approaching a client for the first time, *Dear Mr ... / Yours sincerely*, and when e-mailing a client company, where you don't know the reader's name, then *Dear Sir/Madam / Yours faithfully*. Some companies prefer staff to use a more formal approach, particularly in external e-mails, but others are less formal, and many less traditional phrases are now being seen, e.g. *Dear Mr Smith / (With) best wishes / Kind regards*, etc. In informal e-mails, particularly in the US, greetings like *Martin:* (with no corresponding ending) are becoming more common.

Practice
1   1 c   2 a   3 e   4 g   5 d   6 b   7 f
2   1   I am writing in reply to your letter dated 5 June (*or* June 5).
    2   I look forward to receiving your reply.
    3   Please find attached a copy of our catalogue.
    4   Thank you for your e-mail.
    5   If you have any questions, please do not hesitate to contact me. (*or* Please do not hesitate to contact me if you have any questions.)
    6   I am writing concerning the product launch next week.
    7   I'm really glad to hear about the interview.
    8   Just wondered if you would like to meet up later.
3   1 Dear   2 with   3 to   4 could   5 look
    6 hearing   7 sincerely
4   *Suggested answer*
    To: m.piggott@iut.com
    From: f.close@iut.com
    Cc: k.maskell@iut.com
    Subject: Today's marketing seminar
    Dear Martin
    This is just a quick e-mail to say that Mary won't be able to attend the marketing seminar today. She asked if you could give her a call on her mobile afterwards – she says you have the number.
    Best wishes
    Fiona
5   *Suggested answer*
    Subject: Meeting Mr Franklin
    Dear Mr Ronneberg
    Further to your e-mail of 3rd March, I wish to confirm that I would very much like to meet Mr Franklin next week. Would Tuesday be convenient?
    In addition, please could you send me your specialist brochure on frost-free freezers, if you have one, together with details of your standard payment terms.
    Yours sincerely
    Lars Hansen

Review
1   who needs to receive/see a copy of the e-mail; what you expect them to do; how urgent it is; whether any other information needs to be attached
2   1 Thank you for   2 I would like to   3 let me know
    4 Yours sincerely
3   *Suggested answer*
    Dear Mike
    Nice to hear from you yesterday. I just wondered if you'd like to have lunch today. What about 1.30 in Brown's Bistro? Please give me a call later on to let me know. I'll be in the office all day.
    Best wishes
    Callum
4   See Reference section on page 14.

Unit 2

Transcripts

2.1
Hello, this is José García speaking. Er, as you know, I'm going to be on leave for a week from tomorrow. Could you do me a favour while I'm away? Er, please could you send an e-mail to all the production staff to inform them of investment planned

for the Valencia plant and the implications of this. There are some notes on my desk, by the way. Er, thanks very much. I'll see you when I get back.

2.2

Hi, it's Martine here. I'm going to be out of the office all day. Please could you e-mail Martin Kilsby the production report for the last quarter? The file's in the usual RTP folder on the server. Thanks. Could you mention that Zürich's disappointing rates are because of problems with the old equipment they've got, and that Geneva's rates are twice as high as those in Lucerne due to the new recruitment policy? Finally, some Basel staff will be moving to Lucerne when their factory closes ... probably by July. Er, thanks, goodbye.

Answer key

Context
A results; meeting   B software   C report

Presentation
1 a 1 B   2 A   3 C   4 not used
  b

	Advantages	Disadvantages
1	• good for short e-mails • helps keep the thread	• can lead to lengthy e-mails
2	• good for longer e-mails • helps make the e-mail easier to follow/less confusing	• too little context can lead to misunderstandings
3	• lets the reader see early on what is required of them (to delete, file, respond, etc.) • easier for people who preview messages – only have to read first 5–6 lines to know what the e-mail is about	• people may prefer following information as attachment (easier to file, etc.)
4	• enables you to keep the formatting of a document (e.g. PDF) • saves you from putting a lot of information in the body of an e-mail	• can contain viruses • some companies block all e-mails with attachments or those over a certain size (e.g. 50K) • large attachments may take a long time to receive or block someone's e-mail in-box

4 1 Friedrichshafen has risen by more than 25% compared to the last quarter; Production rates at the Karlsruhe factory were 15% lower than in the previous quarter; the Baden plant plans to increase production from March onwards
  2 This is as a direct result of ...; This fall is due to ...; These problems have led to ...; Finally, in response to ... ; This means that ...
5 See Reference section on page 22.
7 See Reference section on page 22.

Practice
1 1 Firstly, the company plans to invest € 5 million in new machinery.
  2 Secondly, production rates have increased by 25%.
  3 Thirdly, there is growing demand for our products.
  4 Finally, the company has decided to take on 100 new staff.
  5 Firstly, there has been a change to the company's policy.

  6 Finally, $100,000 will be invested in product development.
2 *Suggested answers*
  1 This is due to difficulties we are experiencing with the new machinery.
  2 This is as a result of delays installing the new machinery.
  3 ... which will mean that our production capacity will be higher.
  4 This will probably lead to short-term disruption to production.
  5 This is in response to an increased demand for our latest products.
  6 Owing to the sudden increase in demand for Model XE12, ...
  7 Because of the increased investment, ...
3 1 below   2 attached   3 between   4 paragraph   5 after   6 information
4 *Suggested answers*
  1 Thank you for your phone call. This is just to confirm that I'll send the e-mail you asked me to while you're away. Best regards, Louise
  2 To all staff
  I am writing on behalf of Production Manager José García to confirm two things.
  Firstly, HQ has agreed to a € **50 million expansion** of the main plant here in Valencia. This will mean that the factory will be three times its current size and have a higher production capacity. In addition, due to the development, staff will have better facilities and there will be an improved goods despatch area.
  Secondly, the company plans to open **six new factories** in Spain, which will lead to the creation of at least 150 new jobs. More factories also means the company can manufacture a wider range of products.
  Please see José García for further information.
  Best regards
  Louise Davies

Review
1 department, line, report, capacity
2 1 Firstly, the investment is higher than expected.
  2 Secondly, our production targets are 15% lower than last year.
  3 Finally, production rates in Shanghai/Beijing are as high as those in Beijing/Shanghai.
  4 This is in response to a rise in production.
  5 The changes will lead to an increase in production capacity.
3 The e-mail should say: ***old*** production equipment; ***twice as high as*** those in Lucerne; close by ***July***.
4 *Suggested answer*
  Dear Mr Joekel
  As requested in your e-mail of 22nd February, I am writing to inform you of changes to company policy confirmed by Martin Kilsby.
  1 The production of Model 364 will **move overseas** next year. This will mean that production costs will fall by up to two-thirds.
  2 As a result of more clients wanting to place orders over the Internet, **$1 million** will be invested in the company's website.
  3 The company has decided to sell all its products **in euros** from April onwards. This means that all our systems will have to be updated and clients will need to be informed.
  If you have any questions about the above, please contact me directly for further information.
  Best regards
  Jessie Walker

Unit 3

3.1

Fiona So, Pierre. I hope you've settled in well.

Pierre Yes, I think so, but there's so much to learn ...

F Anything I can help you with?

P Well, there is something ... I've just received an e-mail to say I have to meet the AM tomorrow in F102. What does *AM* mean and what does *F102* stand for?

F Yes, it's confusing isn't it! *AM* means Account Manager – that'll be Bernard Malin – and *F102* stands for Finance 102 – or rather, Room 102 in the Finance building. It's just opposite A Block ...

P Er ... and that is?

F Sorry! That's the administration building over there.

P I see!

Answer key

Context

1 No: she is asking whether Peter can attend a meeting on 21st instead, but there is a lot of superfluous information and repetition.

2 No: the subject line is not filled in, and we don't know what the pronoun *it* refers to.

3 *Dear, Thank, assistant*

4 No, the date isn't specified (just says *next month*).

5 financial advisor, clerical assistant, legal secretary

Presentation

1 3 E-mail E is the clearest: A would be clearer if it had less repetition and irrelevant information. It would also help to have a subject line and for jargon/acronyms to be explained. The reader of B would need *it* explaining, especially as there is no subject line to help; similarly, the reader of D would need clarification of when the interviews are, as *next month* is too vague. C is currently difficult to read as the text is wrapped; it is important to consider the clarity of the layout when writing e-mails, as the writer of E has. In this e-mail, the bullets guide the reader to the key points.

2 2 sentences   3 paragraphs   4 length   6 consistent
7 jargon   8 linking   9 repetition   11 subject
12 italics   13 graphics

4 1 b   2 a

5 1 to give an example, for instance, for example, such as
  2 that is to say, this stands for, this means that, in other words, to put it another way, that is

6 1 *id est* (= that is)   2 *exampli gratia* (= for example)
3 regarding   4 as soon as possible   5 limited
6 per person / pages   7 value added tax
8 public limited company

7 I think it's a really good idea.

8 a See the Reference section on page 30 for suggested answers.
  b Adding: *and, in addition*
    Contrasting: *but, despite, although, however*

Practice

1 *Suggested answers*
  1 To give an example, many of them forgot to include both their school and university qualifications.
  2 This means that we'll have to use one of the smaller meeting rooms.
  3 ... such as last month's sales figures.
  4 For instance, most of our staff are able to attend.
  5 To put it another way, they are all very well qualified.
  6 The meeting's in Block P, which stands for 'production'.
  7 There's a lot on the agenda tomorrow, for example staff recruitment and retention.

2 1 one   2 them   3 Normally   4 now   5 Because
6 this

3 *Suggested answer*
The interview's on 21st September at the Leofric Hotel in Coventry city centre. I'm not worrying about it yet!

4 1 despite   2 also   3 However   4 In addition
5 Although

5 *Suggested answer*

To: P.Matthews@IGR.com
From: J.Daws@IGR.com
Subject: meeting on 15th July
Dear Peter
I'm afraid that, due to another commitment, I will have to postpone the sales meeting planned for tomorrow. Please could you let me know if 21st July would suit you instead?
Best wishes
June

7 *Suggested answer*
Dear Gill
I am afraid that I will not now be able to meet on 3rd May to discuss my work on the Financial Planning project. I am, however, available towards the end of that week, that is Thursday 4th or Friday 5th May. Would either of these alternative days suit you?
Best wishes
Lucy

Review

1 1 Keep   2 Make   3 Avoid   4 Give   5 Use

2 1 They   2 because   3 It   4 meeting
5 Such/These   6 decide

3 *Suggested answer*
Before you can sign up for an online course, you need to register with LearnBusiness.net
To do this:
● Get a registration form from the LearnBusiness.net website at: http://www.lb.net or your local business forum. (For a full list of forums, telephone our hotline on 0194 3845930; open 9–5.30, seven days a week).
● Complete the form in black ink, sign it and return it to:
LearnBusiness.net
36 Primrose Drive
Masden MT12 9YR
(Fill in a **separate** form for each course you are applying for.)
● You will receive a registration card **two to three** days after you register.

5 a AM = account manager; F102 = Room 102 in the Finance building; A Block = Administration block
  b *Suggested answer*
    You have been invited to meet Bernard Malin, the Account Manager, at two o'clock tomorrow afternoon. The meeting will take place in Room 102 in the finance building, opposite the administration building.

Unit 4

4.1

Well, in my opinion, it's important to consider your purpose for writing and who you're writing to. For example, are you writing to someone in the same company or in another company? What relationship do you have with the recipient? You also need to bear in mind what level of formality is appropriate in the culture of the person you're writing to – and, of course, how he or she expects, or prefers, to be addressed.

4.2

Hello, this is Simon Pascalle – P-A-S-C-A-DOUBLE L-E. I'm calling from JHT Limited about an order I placed on 24th January. That was seven weeks ago, but the order hasn't arrived yet. Er, the order number was 124234 ... it was for 26 computer monitors and 15 keyboards. Please could you let me know when it will be delivered. Thanks. Goodbye.

4.3

I don't know what impression Qing thinks his e-mail is giving – of himself and the company – but it's certainly not a very professional one! It looks more like something you'd send to a friend than to a new client you're trying to impress.

Answer key

Context

1 C   2 A   3 B

Presentation

1 1 a   Informal features might include: contractions (*I'm ...*); short sentences; notes/incomplete sentences (*Got your order today ...*); informal subject line (*hi there*); informal punctuation (exclamation marks, dashes); Internet abbreviations/smileys/emoticons; multi-word verbs/idiomatic expressions (*Can you get in touch ...*); informal vocabulary (*stuff ...*); informal grammar (*Can ...*); no (or informal) salutations/closings (*hi!*)

b   Formal features might include: the use of the passive (*It is recommended ...*) rather than I (*I recommend ...*) when representing the company (*we* is also used instead of *I* in more formal e-mails) (note that the passive is also used to be more polite or indirect (see Unit 5)); standard phrases (*If you require ...*); more formal punctuation (colons, semi-colons); more formal grammar (*could ...*); longer and more complex sentences; use of more formal linking phrases (*in addition, however ...*); formal salutations (*Dear Ms ...*). Note that phrases such as *find enclosed herewith* or *should you deem it ...* are considered overly formal in today's business communication.

2   See Transcript 4.1.

3 1 A   2 C   3 B

5 A (informal) Thanks for ..., Thanks a lot!
B (formal) Could/Would you ... ?
C (formal) I have pleasure in confirming ... (informal) Will ...
D (informal) I'm really sorry ...

6 order, run out of, goods, dispatched

7 See Unit 1, Presentation Exercise 8

8 1 too late   2 as far as I know   3 in other words
4 thanks in advance   5 bye for now   6 see you
7 see you later   8 on the other hand   9 thanks
10 for your information   11 by the way
12 frequently asked questions

Practice

1 1 I wish to confirm that your order has been processed.
2 Could I place an order by phone, please?
3 I apologize for the delay to your order.
4 Thank you for your order.
5 Could you confirm your contact details, please?

2 1 'm really sorry   2 a lot   3 got   4 get in touch with
5 let you know; stuff

3 1 d   2 f   3 b   4 c   5 e   6 i   7 g   8 h   9 a

4 1 We would appreciate it if you could provide us with further details of the discounts you offer.
2 A stationery order is placed once a month.
3 The order will be cancelled as soon as possible.
4 We apologize for any inconvenience this may cause.

5 *Suggested answer*
Dear Malle
Thanks so much for helping out this morning. I'd never

have managed to process all those orders on my own! Can you help out tomorrow morning too, by any chance?
Best wishes
Sophia

6 a   Name: Simon Pascalle
Company: JHT Ltd
Order no: 124234
Order details: 26 monitors, 15 keyboards

b   *Suggested answer*
Subject: order no. 124234
Dear Mr Pascalle
I would like to apologize for the delay in dispatching the 26 monitors (model XS243) and 15 keyboards (model RH439) you ordered on 24th January. I wish to confirm that your order left the warehouse this morning and will reach you by 5 p.m. today. I apologize for any inconvenience caused.
Yours sincerely
Kim Hill

7 1 ✔   2 been   3 did   4 to   5 most   6 who   7 ✔
8 many   9 ✔   10 more   11 very

8 There is a mixture of formal and informal expressions in the e-mail. The following changes would make it more consistently formal:
Thanks a lot ➔ *Thank you very much*
Give me a call, will you ➔ *Please call me*
TIA ➔ *Thank you in advance*

Review

1 1 I look forward to receiving your order.
2 If you would like any further information, please do not hesitate to contact me. *or* Please do not hesitate to contact me if you would like any further information.
3 VAT is included in the price.
4 We apologize for any inconvenience caused.
5 I have pleasure in confirming that your order has been dispatched.
6 I am attaching a copy of our updated price list.
7 I just wanted to let you know I've sent the order.
8 Can you get in touch as soon as possible?

2 | *Formal* | *Informal* |
| --- | --- |
| to contact | to get in touch |
| satisfactory | OK |
| to receive | to get |
| very much | a lot |
| to require | to need |
| goods | stuff |
| to dispatch | to send |
| to regret | to be sorry |

3 *Suggested answer*
Dear Mr Martin
Thank you for your order, which I received today. I wish to confirm that the goods will be dispatched immediately.
Yours sincerely
Qing Wan

4 *Suggested answer*
Dear Mr Rajala
I am writing to confirm that we have received your order today. I regret, however, that we do not currently have the requested blue folders in stock. I would be grateful if you could confirm that red folders would be a suitable replacement.
If you require any further information, please do not hesitate to contact me.
Yours sincerely
Lauren Major

Unit 5

Transcripts

5.1

1 Would you believe it? I've just asked my boss for some time off to go to a conference – just look at her reply – it's all in capitals. People say capitals look like you're being shouted at – and I can tell you, that's just how I feel!

2 I got an e-mail yesterday from a colleague I'd offered to help with his business trip. Talk about an ungrateful reply. I won't bother offering next time!

3 I don't like being given orders, and 'sort it out' certainly sounds like an order, don't you think? Aren't some people rude?

5.2

Hi, it's Petra here. I've just heard that Michael Laker ... er, from the Margate branch ... is coming for a meeting next week. Could you please send him an e-mail for me and see whether he can make Tuesday – and if he wants us to book overnight accommodation for him on the Monday? Many thanks.

Answer key

Context

1 B   2 C   3 A

Presentation

3 2 anyone throughout the world   3 any body language
4 your purpose   5 you are shouting
6 get someone to check your e-mail first
7 between colleagues   8 sensitive

4 a 1 C   2 A   3 B
   b 1 B   2 C   3 A   4 B   5 B   6 C   7 A   8 B   9 A
      10 C

5 1a The use of the imperative *Sort out* ... makes the first sentence in the pair the most direct; it sound like an order.

   2a The use of *Would you mind ... + -ing?* makes the second sentence in the pair the most indirect and polite.

6 You may wish the tone of your writing to be strong, neutral or tentative. *Highly* and *completely* are used in sentences 4 and 7 to help the writers express their views strongly, i.e. not just recommending, but giving a strong recommendation; not just agreeing, but agreeing 100%. *Fairly* (sentence 2) is used to be more tentative, i.e. that the airport could be seen as modern, but not as modern as all that!
Might (sentence 3) is also used to be tentative, i.e. that the writer is only about 50% sure he'll pick the person up.
Probably (sentence 5) is also used to show the writer is not 100% sure that the colleague is meeting up for lunch – only about 70% sure.
By using *not very* + a positive adjective (sentence 6), rather than using a negative adjective, the writer can be less direct and might come across as less abrupt or rude to the reader.
Should (sentence 7) is used for giving advice; *must* is much stronger and indicates obligation.
Note that what is seen as being direct/less direct differs between cultures.

Practice

1 *Suggested answers*
   1 Could you book me a single room with an ensuite bathroom, please?
   2 Would you send me your latest hotel brochure, please?
   3 Can you please arrange for a taxi to pick me up from the airport at 10.30 on Monday?
   4 Would you mind cancelling my flight?
   5 Would you leave us your contact details for Paris before you leave, please?

   6 The hotel bill doesn't seem to have been paid.
   7 Would it be possible to have a room with a view, please?
   8 I would be grateful if you could confirm my reservation by faxing me on 00 43 485 39489.

2 1 entirely   2 very   3 far   4 highly   5 quite   6 really
   7 much   8 definitely

3 *Suggested answers*
   1 Everyone here must start work at eight.
   2 People should phone in if they are off sick.
   3 We can leave early if we tell our boss the day before.
   4 You might like to ask for a tour of the building.
   5 We could meet up tomorrow if you like.

4 1 e   2 d   3 f   4 b   5 a   6 c

5 *Suggested answers*
   A It looks like there might be a mistake, as I asked for a room with a shower, not a bath. Would you mind sorting it out? Thanks.
   B I'd rather you didn't, because we're rather busy then. Another day that week would be fine, though.
   C It's very kind of you to offer, but I don't actually need any help at the moment, thank you.

6 *Suggested answer*
   Dear Michael
   Petra tells me that you are coming for a meeting next week. Could you possibly make Tuesday? If so, would you like us to book overnight accommodation for you on the Monday night? Please confirm if this is convenient for you, and let me know your accommodation requirements.
   Best regards
   Jérôme Gillet

7 1 I'll pick up the clients if you like.
   2 Could you cancel my hotel reservation for me?
   3 Would it be possible to change my flight?
   4 Would you mind helping me with the report?
   5 I'd rather you didn't take your holiday now.

8 E-mail 1: g, f, a, e, h, m, i
   E-mail 2: j, k, l, b, c, d

Review

1 1 Would you like me to call a taxi?
   2 Could you confirm the time of your arrival?
   3 Would you mind if I took a later flight?
   4 I'd like to speak to the tour guide.
   5 May I have your booking reference please?
   6 Shall I book the hotel accommodation?

2 May I ...? Could I ...? Is it OK if I ...? I want to ...

3 *Suggested answer*
   Dear Bernd
   Would you book me a return ticket to Frankfurt on 18th August, please? I would be grateful if you could send it to my home address by Friday, if possible.
   Best wishes
   Hari

4 1 trip   2 flight   3 accommodation   4 single
   5 ensuite

5 See the Reference section on page 46.

Unit 6

Transcripts

6.1

F Hello, Higgs Communications. How can I help you?
M I'd like to register for your 'Online' training course – the one in Paris next month.
F Certainly, can I take your name?
M It's Qing – that's Q-I-N-G – Wan, from MYT International.
F Thank you, Mr Wan. As it's close to the event, I'll have to send you the full registration form by e-mail ... you can fill it in electronically and mail it back. There have also been

some changes to the programme. Was it the full three days you wanted to attend?

M No, just Thursday and Friday.

F OK, I'll ask my assistant to send you the programme for those two days. Can I just take your e-mail address?

M Yes, it's ...

6.2

M Hi, Leigh. Glad I've bumped into you ... The sales training event is going to have to be rescheduled, from 13th April to 15th March.

F Oh?

M Someone's overbooked the venue.

F I see. So will it be the same time – eleven to five?

M We're going to start a bit earlier – half past ten – so we should finish half an hour earlier, too. Could you let Diane know?

F Sure.

6.3

Hi. I'm not going to be in till about twelve. Could you e-mail Jane for me and thank her for the e-mail? She said the sales meeting is today, but I have tomorrow at ten in my diary ... Also, she said we were in the boardroom, but I have booked Room 343. Perhaps you could let her know. Thanks.

Answer key

Presentation

1 1 Mr Qing Wan   2 Participation in a training course in Paris   3 A registration form and the programme

2 No, the caller receives information for Friday only; information for Thursday and Friday was requested. He may need to clarify the dates (different on the programme and the e-mail; whether there are any changes to Thursday's programme; which workshop has been cancelled).

3 Neither is very accurate. See Practice Exercise 11 for an amended version.

Practice

1 a Event: sales training event
      Date: 15th March
      Time: 10.30 a.m. – 4.30 p.m.

2 16th March ➜ 15th March; eleven ➜ ten thirty; five ➜ four thirty

3 1 *principle* = noun (*rule/belief*); *principal* = adjective (*main*)
   2 *interesting* = adjective (describes an object); *interested* = adjective (describes a person's attitude)
   3 *personal* = adjective (*concerning an individual*); *personnel* = noun (*staff*)
   4 *valuable* = adjective (*having worth*); expensive = adjective (*costing a lot of money*)
   5 *eventually* = adverb (*after a long time*); *finally* = adverb (*last in a series*)
   6 *become* = verb (*turn into*); *receive* = verb (*get*)
   7 *trainer* = noun (*someone who gives training*); *trainee* = noun (*someone who receives training*)
   8 *however* = adverb (used to add a surprising or contradictory piece of information); *although* = conjunction (*despite the fact that*)

4 1 valuable   2 personnel   3 However   4 trainer
   5 Finally   6 received   7 interested

5
	American English	British English
1	canceled	cancelled
2	center	centre
3	color	colour
4	organize	organise
5	license	licence
6	practice	practise
7	traveler	traveller
8	labor	labour
9	theater	theatre

6 There are three parts to the course: finance, marketing and HR. Mark Draper will be the main trainer for the finance and marketing sessions; Joy Marlow will be responsible for HR. Do you have any questions about the course content?

7 1 I have lived here **for** two years.
   2 If I **had** more time, I would take a course.
   3 I **think** that we should postpone the next training course.
   4 We haven't had **many** participants on the courses.
   5 The trainer **did** his best to motivate all the participants.
   6 We all look forward **to** seeing you soon.
   7 There's been a **significant** increase in the course cost.

8 *Suggested answers*
   1 participants.   2 finish the report.
   3 I would leave my job.   4 1995.
   5 should have regular breaks.   6 to meeting you.
   7 fall in demand.

9 1 am writing   2 take   3 which   4 on   5 Doing
   6 have   7 advice   8 to contact   9 hearing
   10 sincerely

10 1 'm attending / will be attending   2 it's   3 If you're
    4 meet   5 going   6 for   7 like   8 make

11 *Suggested answer*
    Thank you for registering for the 'Online Training for Business' conference, **which** is taking place in Paris from **8–10 October**.
    I have attached the final conference **programme** for **Thursday and** Friday as you **requested**. **Please note** that there **aren't** any last-minute amendments to the **itinerary** for **Wednesday** and Thursday, but there are a **few** for Friday.
    On Friday, the plenary **starts** at eleven o'clock and will be in Room 311. The workshop **at 13:00** has been cancelled, as the **principal** speaker is ill.

12 a E-mail Jane about the sales meeting.
       Date: tomorrow
       Time: 10 a.m.
       Place: Room 343
    b *Suggested answer*
       Dear Jane
       This is just a quick e-mail to let you know that Sam left a voicemail message about the sales meeting. Apparently it's taking place at 10 a.m. tomorrow in Room 343 and not today in the boardroom.
       Best wishes
       Sandra

Review

1 *Suggested answers*
   1 six months.   2 training courses.
   3 am attending a finance course.   4 I would leave my job.
   5 seeing you next week.   6 book that is?
   7 contact me if you require additional information.
   8 complaints about the course so far.

2 1 b   2 a   3 c   4 h   5 d   6 e   7 f   8 g

3 1 Although   2 who   3 seeing   4 interested   5 it's
   6 many

4 Thank you for your e-mail **inviting** me to be your plenary speaker at the 'Sales Direct' conference in London ~~in~~ next month. I would be **delighted** to accept your invitation. However, I **would be** very grateful if you could let me know as soon **as** possible when exactly the conference is taking place, in which centre and what I should speak about.